Conversations

with my

Son

Conversations

with my

Mother

*An in-depth look
at ordinary things*

Jeannette Caruth and
Quinten Caruth

Cover image is Copyright ©
iStock.com with credit to
iStock.com/boule13

ISBN: 978-0-578-31491-4 (sc)
ISBN: 978-0-578-31492-1 (hc)
ISBN: 978-0-578-31493-8 (e)

Contents

Introduction	v
Daily Activities	1
Waiting	7
Seeing	11
Gratitude	15
Mystery	20
Pain	26
OK-ness	34
Past	39
Inspiration	44
The Tides	50
Grace	57
Intention	78
Endurance	84
Dreams	92
Elements/Senses	99
Do's and Don'ts	107
Tendernes	116
Escape	123
Poetry	131
The Folly of Age	139
Confidence	147
Life	162

Introduction

Mother:

I feel like writing... actually I always feel like writing. Time and circumstances have a tendency to stack up around me and the moments fleet away. Yet, the desire is so unmistakably here and loudly so. Not exactly sure what to write, it made me wonder and search more deeply for a direction. Endless poems I have written, but now it made me look for something more diligently constant. And so the idea emerged. My son too loves to write, and for him circumstances and time seem to halt him as well from enjoying this delightful, playful creativity. Why not, I thought... don't both of us delve into various topics and share our respective viewpoints. How interesting and fun this could be... my view as a woman of 70 and his view as a man of 41, both deeply connected, but yet in a world with different eyes, different minds, but possibly beating with the same heart... This is my invitation to him, to share this exciting journey, flowing from our mother-son entity into a kaleidoscopic landscape of our written thoughts, feelings and emotions. If this calls you, my dearest son... join me...

Son:

Mother... Thank you so much for this invitation. I've written many things that I have never shared with you. At many times in my life, words poured forth from me, unstoppable from a river of emotion or feeling, inspiration, or just plain mystery. I've always been shy to share it, but it is apparent that writing is in my blood. I think it would be foolish to not explore what might possibly lie in the pastures of wonder before us. A part of me resisted doing this, as I felt "who am I to think that anybody would want to read what I write?" But I wasn't looking at the simpler approach, and that is just to write because I want to. Write to see what unfolds. Write to have this beautiful opportunity at a truly unique exchange with my most beloved Mother that might endure for eons. If it is read by others or not, is not so important. I don't need to feel shy or careful about the reasons or results. It's not about that. It's about enjoying seeing what wishes to be expressed through our Mother-Son dynamic, and perhaps turning that "possibly beating with the same heart" into an unmistakable, undeniable realization of our one beating heart. I do join you, and I already love the conjoined journey.

Daily Activities

Mother:

My pen is here, my keyboard is here... but am I here? These two things have one thing in common: once I sit down to use them, there is a white blankness that stares at me. This is when the challenge announces itself. And as always, it begs me to be comfortable with not knowing, to somehow find the silence that the mind brings forward, soothing, and allow it to be. I can feel that the paper or blank screen (less poetic!) quietly urges me to fill it. Looking for a topic, I must stumble upon something... maybe we should venture out into the so-called dreary daily routines, which are not necessarily so dreary and so routine-fixed as we generally believe them to be. Why? For one simple reason: I never performed them before as I performed them today, or will tomorrow... ha... this is actually an exciting discovery! The madness of the thought of a routine is what seems to blind me. Getting up, yawning, trying to get my legs to move, using the

1

bathroom, washing my face – getting a scary glimpse of the reflection in the mirror... and yes... here it is, the impression of a routine returned once more. But, if I look closely, the face is not the same, and with that observation, the thought too is truly slightly different. Hmm... this could be interesting. Going to the kitchen, I grab the coffee to put in the machine, and for a split second I look at the spoon and decide to fill it a little more than yesterday, measuring the water; I wonder if I want to add more water or less water than usual. I try to do the water the same, but now I am really thinking about it... is it the same or did I change it? The coffee machine starts to make its comforting noise and the smell seems equally wonderful as yesterday. The joy of its aroma somehow seems to definitely be new each day..! Does that mean that whatever is delightful makes the routine lose its negative tone? Quite possibly so, I think. I try to make the breakfast also slightly differ from the day before. Pondering about all this while taking my first sips and bites has started my day off on a new adventure. Maybe the routine has as its only purpose for me to discover that there really is not such a thing as a routine, it is just a thought that we have made into a sort of ugly thing. Being super bored with doing dishes, I frantically look for another approach to this endlessly recurring activity. I realize that the boredom with it really starts when I am sort of lost in my thoughts... but if I just simply try to put a new edge on it, it seems that I can break that cycle. Suddenly, I destroy the monotonous dread of it by paying attention to doing it consciously different than yesterday. And so I venture out into the rest of the day – showering, getting dressed, starting the car, driving, and running errands; It becomes obvious that it is just my thought of a routine that creates the only obstacle. I can make it as much fun as I want to... not so much as in looking for the superb satisfaction of the reaching a desired result of one activity – but just the discovery of how easy it is to break the cycle of our self-imposed labels on our daily doings. I like it. Of course the tantalizing thought of settling for complaining comes in easily..! I don't know about you... but sometimes it feels simply darn good to complain... it has its own satisfaction. I am deciding to not make it hard on myself and let each day dictate where it will lead me. Or, welcome the laziness of complaining and sort of ironically rest in that - or - venture out on a discovery tour to find the new edges of daily routines and extend them beyond the thought of dreariness... and pour light on it all. I am realizing that it all depends on how much I want to manage the love for life and with that embrace... the love for my own silly self.

Son:

Mother, I'm humbled by your writing. It's breathtakingly beautiful, open, honest, and refreshing. But then, that's how you've always been. In a way, it made me want to reverse roles, be your father, and hold you in my arms, love you, and protect you from the feelings that may creep in of dreary daily routines. The depth that you convey even in these simple daily moments moved me to a deep compassion and love for you; coupled with an admiration for how you approach and attempt to transform the seemingly mundane into something magical. You are magical. There's no doubt about that.

If the subject of this chapter is the approach to daily routines, then I will try to share how my experience is in such circumstances. I can't say that I ever tried to play with these moments as you do. I do love your approach: creating beauty, fun, and joy where others might not notice it. For me, I guess my approach is to fill those experiences with peace. What is my ratio of success with this approach? Probably 50/50. If I observe what is going on inside me while washing dishes, cooking, cleaning, etc., it feels as though I just yearn for the middle road. I try to stay centered within myself, doing the things that need to be done, quietly, without any real thought about it. When successful, I can't say that I find it particularly pleasant nor unpleasant; just peaceful. I guess I find the peace pleasant, but that is regardless of the action being performed.

If I'm being honest and truly observant of the actions, yes, there's a part of me that enjoys cleaning away the dirt, having a clean home, having clean laundry that smells fresh, or a good meal that was crafted well. I like the warm water running over my hands, the smell of the soap, cleaning away the grease of the pans. There are also parts of me that do not look forward to these tasks. But I would say that, largely, the enjoyment or the condemnation of these events is more of a background experience, rather than a foreground one.

Do I complain about these tasks at times? Certainly! Is complaining enjoyable? Of course it is! When we complain, we add a story to a situation or feeling. The mind loves its stories, whether good or bad. That's just simply what it does. I love how you attempt to rosy the picture. You do a damn good job of it! I've never known anybody to be as rosy as you, Mother! My heart explodes with love and admiration for who you are, and how you approach so many things in life. Me, being the Taurean bull, I try to choose the more passive route of chewing my grass slowly. So, I suppose the contrast is that of a passive or active approach. We simply follow that which is natural to our being, and all roads lead home.

And you always have a home in my heart, and I know that I always have a beautiful home in yours.

Poem by son:

With the routines of the day
Time seems to slip and fade
We can engage the moments in play
Or balancing on the razors edge of equanimity,
we can stay
Regardless of the way
There's one thing that I can say
The unlimited options are a vast array
And love is the ultimate power to carry all
burdens away.

Waiting

Mother:

New topic! Yep, here it is, topic number two... thoroughly intimidating are those words, but trust is my guide and walking is my joy. Walking through life, taking one unknown step after another and smilingly looking onto the horizon, where somehow it seems a big smile is always greeting me... how sweet it is. I imagine it is because it's unknown and therefore filled with wonder, a sense of playful awe... the same sense we had as children looking at the wrapped packages under the Christmas tree. We did not know what was in them... but somehow it made us always smile, and therefore, our steps were ever lighter and our hearts beating faster with the anticipation of more joy. In all of that, I can see that basically not-planning has a huge advantage. It leaves my mind still, more at peace, and the spaciousness allows for whatever to unfold. I discovered that with this sort of attitude, at the craziest moments, clarity will announce itself and lead us joyfully on. I am especially thinking back to a moment in time when there was not much going on, and a sense of boredom had set in; nothing to do and again nothing to do and... nothing to do. Looking at that state of mind, it started to feel definitely annoying, and with that, the density of nothing became heavy. What to do... the minutes seem to get longer, the hours more frustrating, and so on. And then the decision came to go to the store to buy some groceries. And the funny thing was... there was a long line of people waiting to get in (during covid time!); my husband and I joined the line and there we stood. But I noticed that all of a sudden, the heavy sense of nothing was replaced by a sense of purpose. This was amazing, because I actually again was doing absolutely nothing!! And that form of nothingness lifted my being and I had to laugh – the nothingness at home on the couch was the same nothingness as in the long line of waiting... but my mind had allowed to let a "meaning" slip in there – and now the nothingness was delightful. Imagine that... how deliciously ridiculous life is... or actually not life, but our mind. I think life is playing hide and seek with me and I just don't realize it..! But guess what... I am catching on! It is about time at 70, don't you think? That is why the adding of years, to me, has been the most wonderful discovery.

Life has become lighter and lighter and now I can play ball with the game of nothingness of Life.

Son:

Waiting

*Let me see, what does this word mean for me,
this waiting?
Internally debating, as I sit and wonder, waiting
for a divine spark of thunder.
Looking for the right words to inspire,
To lift souls like birds, ever higher and higher.
Waiting all my life for something,
it has felt for me.
And as I sit and write this, that finally
feels somewhat free.
There is a natural flow from pen to paper,
The faucet's wide open, a flavor to savor.
Peace fills my soul, as the words enter my mind,
Like the shine of gold, sometimes hard to find.
As I sit and wait for the next line,
It becomes apparent that the words aren't
necessarily mine.
I sit and I trust, writing what comes,
Doing as I must, on this journey of
Mother and Son
I'm writing as I've never done before,*

Just writing the words, not knowing if
there's more.
Where this journey leads, where the path goes?
I just bow on my knees to the One who knows.
What could the outcome of all this be?
I don't know, we'll just have to wait and see...

Seeing

Son:

How often do we actually see things in each day? I'm lying here on my couch, looking out the window, trying to think of the next subject, next chapter of the book. And I see a palm tree... probably a palm tree that I've looked at and walked by a thousand times. But I don't think that I've ever seen it the way that I do now. I'm giving it my attention. I really notice the contrast of the leaves blowing in the wind against the backdrop of the misty blue sky. I see how solid and unwanting it is. Just there, being a tree. And it's beautiful, majestic, peaceful. It's just there, whether you see it or not. Is it just me that rarely sees? Or how do you see the things?

I wonder how many things there are each day that I don't see? Though I try to stay quiet in mind, there is often some type of dialogue, whether it's playing out a story of myself on a talk show with my mom when our book reaches number 1, what questions they might ask me, how will I respond, or any other number of unlimited possibilities that seem to run on automatic in the mind. It seems to kind of leave a persistent fog on the lens of my eyes. Recently, I've thought that maybe I need glasses. But perhaps I just need to see better.

And I wonder how often we see through this fog when looking at our fellow (hu)man? It's a shame. This fog can be limiting. There's a fog in the mind of memories of each person that we know. Any person could have a profound shift in how they view themselves and the world, and somehow be completely new. But when they meet somebody that "knows" them, they won't be seen. They will be seen based on their past patterns and stories. And these beliefs in the eyes of the other could be limiting, pulling back the renewed person to doubt their newfound experience, pulling them back to their old ways. And so, in a way, it could be more freeing to meet new people. People who don't know the former person, and only see them as they are right now. There's a freedom in that. A freedom to express without limits. How often do we truly see who is before us without placing these limits on them? I can't profess to be able to do this myself. Only that I will try to set everybody free from my clouded lens as much as grace allows. How do you see the seeing?

Mother:

Nice subject and oh such a good question: I really like your observation, your conclusion and your intent. Glad you do not need glasses... and with that. I mean to clean the fog from your eyes as our minds try to trick us. Your observation has cleared that up!

Now, you are asking me: "how do I see seeing?" When I delve into that - the first thing that comes to my mind is... I feel. I don't think particularly about the seeing when I look, because I immediately sense the feeling. I so long to feel a connection with the "me" inside, with the object that I'm looking at, that I seem to go for that. I'm not sure if that means I am bypassing something, but that is the immediate response that comes up. So far, I have to confess that I really haven't investigated forms. I sense it more as if the forms are a doorway to my field of inner perception, a way of receiving. It might truly be quite possible that once I will start really looking at forms, and the contrasts around them, with the sky or whatever envelops them, that my sense of perception will deepen. I find it an interesting invitation for observation, and will try this out and see what happens. Thus far it remains an open question. This is to be continued after a few days of "seeing"...

Ok, I am back. I liked it. It brought me a sweet sense of wonder by just letting the forms somehow formlessly enter my eyes. It created more stillness and, I guess, like you said, the fog of immediate labeling took a backdrop. It did indeed deepen the perception. I must hesitantly admit that looking at the trees, nature, mountains, flowers, etc., was a heck of a lot easier than looking at people. Once I tried to just look at the form of their faces, their noses, their eyes, the structure of their bodies, it became a bit more tricky. How easily the mind jumps in and takes over. So far, I have to confess, that with people, I definitely prefer to immediately go into the "feeling" field, rather than just taking in the forms. The way of approaching "seeing" almost feels to me that maybe since my instant response was "I feel first before I actually see," is because I am a woman and I believe that we mostly look for a connection with the heart. That is my starting point and if I am lucky, it remains and will embrace all that I see.

Gratitude

Mother:

Recently, I started this fun exchange with a friend of mine about gratitude. Every morning, we grab paper and pen... haha... nowadays an old concept... I need to rephrase that... we grab the cell phone and start typing out the things we feel grateful for in that first moment after waking up. It is interesting to do, because I also noticed that, amazingly enough, I sometimes wake up and immediately am fogged over and just don't want to look for anything to be grateful for. It seems like an effort and part of me rebels against that. So on days like that, it almost feels like I reach out to the "second row" of stuff and pluck whatever seems to fit. Those become the obvious things... like food in the fridge, some money in the bank, etc., etc. I have to say that after several weeks of doing this... I truly start to realize what the things are that I am most grateful for in this

15

life, at this moment. And with that practice, I must admit the gratitude becomes definitely deeper, and with that, obviously more present. What turns out to be most important to me, is time and again, my surroundings. I totally love and drink in the peaceful environment where I live – the sweet atmosphere in my house – and a sense of connection with the neighborhood. That actually is a bit interesting. I really do not have a lot of contact with the neighbors. They are a mixed bundle from all walks of life, and not always the good walks of life, if you know what I mean. But every morning, I reach out inwardly and embrace the whole sort of community, neighborhood. It is not felt as a "practice," per se... it comes totally natural to do that. I do sincerely embrace them and can feel the joy of that. It feels like throwing a net of love over the whole place and this brings the echo of it back to me, and that is what I love and am so grateful for. Yes... now that I think about it... it is the "echo" that makes me happy. I can see now that gratitude calls forth this sense of ok-ness and it spreads around into our field, and as it flows out further and further – it cannot help but come back to us... maybe like a boomerang, but I prefer the word echo. It has a deeper resonance for me. In other words, gratitude is the call for the Joy of Life – it matters little what I am grateful for. Nonetheless, it is such a fun way to discover what touches me most. This funny thing happened today, and I believe it is caused by this practice with my friend. Without even consciously trying to find things to be grateful for... I sort of start to hum with joy about those common everyday things that we take for granted... I suddenly felt deeply grateful for turning a switch on and see the light come on... wow... this is amazing!! After that, I turned on the stove... and yep, there it was, and I could start cooking. Even opening a door became interesting, and feeling grateful for the one who invented such a magnificent object that makes life easier for us... and endless becomes the list and sweeter every time, the echo...

I am grateful for being grateful
for hearing the Echo
and feeling the Joy of Life...

Son:

I can't have a chapter about gratitude without first expressing my gratefulness that you are my Mother. I wouldn't be who I am without you. Thank you.

It's interesting that you should choose the word gratitude on this day as the subject of the next chapter. We must be in some kind of harmonious synchronicity. I think I've heard this word more times today than on any other day in *my life! It has come up several times today with a friend of mine. We have been sharing a lot of deep discussions, outlooks, insights, and writings. And for whatever reason, today seemed to be a day of immense gratitude for this sharing and being thankful for the equally encouraged upliftment of each other's spirit. And we both seem to be entering into a state of greater surrender to an unseen flow of life that keeps dropping sweet little hints at the path that lies ahead. And it seems that the more that we relax into this current of the natural way, the more splendorous become the gifts. Even without necessarily working so diligently on any "spiritual practice," per se, the simple act of trying to listen, trying to feel this guidance, has already caused enormous changes in my overall being. The peace gets deeper and more vast, the heart burns as if the petals of love are opening faster than might be expected, and that which seemed before impossible, no longer seems to be out of reach. In fact, things that I might have never even imagined were possible before are now kind of funny to me. I find it funny that I doubted anything at all. Because I can feel the unlimited potential there, and I can see that it is only the mind that attempts to limit that freedom for fear that it will burn in the fire of constant, unceasing blessings and love that fall upon the road of the unwavering, patient, and trusting heart.*

I see now that when I tried to do life, I wasn't doing it so well. But when I allow life with greater and greater authority to lead me, my God... the gifts never stop coming! There is beauty at every turn, love enough to consume all past pains, a silent peace that reverberates in all directions. Life is infinitely more beautiful when we allow it to carry us and reveal its treasures. And my heart has never known such gratitude. Gratitude for the endless and deepening blessings that are showered upon my fateful path. I don't know which direction the path goes, but I pray to be humble enough to never go deaf to its sweet calling, and that I may spend the rest of my days in this field of wonder and gratitude.

Mystery

Mother:

Since childhood, I have always loved that word. It sounds so inviting, and yet, it totally shuts one up. It leaves one dumbfounded, yet not in a senseless way. It actually keeps me immensely alive and I would say very alert. I would like to compare it to the feeling I have when I go to a theater and am waiting for the curtain to open up. One knows nothing of what is behind it... and once the bells ring to announce that the play will commence – there suddenly is a deep silence. It is truly a reverberating silence. I can feel the intense collective expectation of the audience. It is that pristine alertness which I could define as the mystery. And now that I think of it... the very same feeling of mystery is what grabs me when I am the one behind the curtain waiting to go on stage! Every time when my man and I are about to start our flamenco show, we look at each other and we know that with all of our good intentions, we truly have no idea how the next hour will unfold. At this time, I must admit that that kind of mystery does not leave me with a deep sense of peace... haha... no, in all honesty... it leaves me with the familiar butterflies in the stomach, but somehow I still totally treasure the not knowing of what the mystery will bring me. Yep... there are so many ways of describing it. There is, for instance, also the incredible unfolding of the mystery of my life. The immaculate timing of each movement and motion during my 70 years. The orchestration of that majestic magic has to leave one speechless. This is also, for me, an enormous advantage of having lived many years on this marvelous planet Earth. It opens up the softening of resistance. I love bringing this awareness into any kind of situation. Don't laugh, but I do this all the time, and in a sense (am definitely a bit nuts), it is almost fun to invite a bit of resistance into silly moments just to feel more of how the mystery actually takes control of everything. Take for instance today... I was very busy and felt actually quite eager to sit down, peacefully, at my keyboard (I'm learning to drop the phrase pen and paper!). I felt myself hurrying through the doings of the day, and the cooking of the meals, etc. By the time I had to clean up, my sense of resistance started to throw punches at me. Ah, I thought... I wonder how the *magic of the day will unfold. Because as for right now, I do not see any "peaceful" moment ahead of me, with plenty more chores to take care of and my man being around needing attention for various issues. Not fighting my new-born inward struggle... I watch both this inner stormy field and the outer field of circumstances. And then... there it was: all of a sudden, out of the clear blue sky, my man decided to go do a chore that he had just done not too long ago. There was no need for it, and normally he doesn't leave in the afternoon; but now, suddenly he got up and left the house for me to be alone! The call was clear... here I am – totally in peace, and enjoying every word that seems to love the touch of the keyboard to become a tangible form. I meet Mystery at every turn and invite Her in as often as I remember Her.*

I once wrote a poem about Her and here it is:

The Miracle

*Inexplicable... unexplainable...
this day finds me with deep feelings,
bottomless feelings,
endlessly reaching out
to an ever expanding horizon,
and in its worldly expression,
one calls it Love...
yet... the masquerade of this word*

does not do this feeling justice.
It is love, peace, and joy all in one,
and each component of it has its
equal in the other.
Wordlessly I sit in it
as words flow out from it,
a gentle swaying to its melody
allows me to call it
a harmonious divine sense of well-being,
a return to the womb of a truthful reality.
Here, tomorrows and yesterdays meet,
today remains.
Silence reigns, yet sings,
and in the echo of its sound, I dwell.
Inexplicably so, unexplainable
I am this and so are you.
Such is the wonder of being.

Son:

If I tune in to this word "mystery," and what it means for me, I feel this field of unlimited possibilities reverberating through each and every atom of each and every thing as well as the space that encompasses all those things. It feels as if each fiber in the carpet below my feet, as well as each sound that I hear, has some element of mystery waiting to be unlocked. Nothing truly seems ordinary. There is a taste of the mysterious in everything, all the time. What a pity that as

23

adult humans, we become so comforted with our knowledge, that we miss the mysteriousness that peeks at us from all angles. I can remember as a child being so curious about everything. "Mom, what is that? Why does it do that? Where does it come from? How is it made? And why, but why Mom... and why that?" The world was a magical place, eagerly awaiting discovery. The mind ran rampant with imaginative stories, and limits were not so perceivable. As time passes, we feel comfortable in the structures that we have built up that serve to make sense of the world around us. We feel supported in the comfort of our mental framework. I guess, over time, maybe we become afraid of the mysterious? As it may not seem to have any ground of support there. But I don't remember feeling afraid of the mysteries of life as a child... more curious, excited, and inquisitive than fearful. But it is difficult to feel too much fear when you know that you have the unconditionally loving lap of your Mother for which to rest your head and feel ultimate comfort and support; giving courage to go forth and explore the unknown, knowing that she is always there to give a guiding hand, a kind word, or a complete cloud of love for which to rest your weary soul.

So, do we gradually fear the mysterious, or do we just stop noticing it once we've "learned" enough information to explain it away? I'm not *sure, but I believe that the notion that the mysterious has no ground of support is an incorrect one. For the secrets of creation lie in that mystery. That incomparable, unimaginable sweet mystery that would appear to be hiding, but only to the mind. But once we tap into it, feel into it, sense it, we find that this mystery is actually quite familiar, and is the ultimate ground for which to stand upon. Nothing can shake one who stands upon this ground. And even though this mystery seems familiar, it never loses its mysteriousness. In fact, it seems to become paradoxically more mysterious the more familiar it becomes. It's like a divine nectar, and with each drop, new levels of mystery and experience are revealed, leaving one in awe of its endless revelations, opening one to a renewed childlike wonder once again. There is mystery everywhere, always, just waiting eternally to be heard, unlocked, and allowed to demonstrate its never-ending splendor. It's as unconditionally patient and loving as a Mother. It never forces attention upon itself. And it never goes away. It's endlessly there, calling silently from within and without... like a warm blanket, always available to comfort those that might have lost their way in the imagined comforts of the mind and forgotten the beauty of the mysteries that are revealed to the innocent heart. The mystery awaits.*

Pain

Son:

Mother, today my heart hurts. So, I thought if we are to keep this conversation flowing as naturally, openly, and vulnerable as possible, that I might as well not pretend to be immune to pain and go ahead and express its experience through me into the world. The pain in this particular case is related to a soul that has a nearly impossible level of compatibility with my own. Actually, in the first 20 minutes of meeting her, my heart was already burning. I knew that I had encountered a truly deep, innocent, wise, and loving being. The road has already been a rocky one in the month that we have known each other. She has openly spoken of being somewhat terrified of me, and having never felt so vulnerable, in that someone could understand and see them at their deepest levels. And every time that we get a little bit closer, she runs away. With each escape, something happens with such precise timing and "coincidence," that circumstance brings us back to meet again. I can see the tenderness in her eyes. I can feel how afraid she is to reveal just how beautiful, innocent, and huge her heart is. I don't think she ever thought that somebody would notice it. And it terrifies her for that to be exposed. I can see fear there, behind the tenderness, fearing the depth that we might be able to explore. In these moments, I just want to hold her, kiss her, and tell her that everything will be OK. But I also know that if I do that, and open the floodgates of love, that it might overwhelm her. So, I keep patiently holding back, hoping that she will gradually melt and relax into a greater state of trust. Two days ago, we had our first real kiss. It was instantaneous passion, like two parted lovers, separated by decades of misfortune. Our bodies immediately molded into one another in a fire of unity. Even though the magnetic spark was undeniable, I could still feel her fear. I didn't put too much of my heart into it, knowing that it might be too soon, and lead to the next escape. Even so, without explanation, without a goodbye, she disappeared in the morning. I already couldn't sleep as I felt her walls of protection from vulnerable feelings returned, and I fully expected her to run away at any moment. Such a helpless feeling. Wanting her to stay, but also not wanting to hold her back, or not even wanting energetically to restrict her freedom to go. So, I pretended to be sleeping when I heard her go, even though it was breaking my heart. I'm 41 years old. I have had 4 significant relationships. One was with a truly innocent and tender, childlike at times, being. Another was with an intensely sensual creature. A third was a deeply spiritual soul. And finally, there was one for which love itself was the prominent quality. Each one had something that I was really called to, and admired, but there always seemed as if something didn't quite mesh properly. My soul would become agitated and uneasy, and I'd be the one needing escape. I didn't think that it was possible to encounter someone that had all the qualities that called to my being. And now that I've found such a rare treasure, she keeps running away. Haha! I guess it's my turn to be run away from. But this particular distancing after our last meeting seems as though it might be final. The intensity of feelings that we shared seems to have caused a level of exposure that she isn't ready to face or share with another soul. And now that we crossed the friendship barrier, it seems that there might not be a way to get back to safer waters in her eyes. And so, the most secure option seems to be to not see me anymore. So, I've lost a friend today. A friend that I've probably shared more of my soul with than any other person. And not for *lack of trying. Nobody has been able to see me the way that she does, in all facets, in all ways, with nothing but tender loving acceptance. I told her things that I've never told anybody else, shared some writing that nobody has ever seen. And there was always only loving encouragement, upliftment, no judgment, and a true honoring of the openness for which I expressed my many dimensions. And she, in kind, returned the favor with a level of honesty that she had not been accustomed to. We both saw each other's so called "dark" and "light" sides with a level of trust that I've never experienced before. We found that the depth that we both have gone and explored in all dimensions of the physical and spiritual realms was equal, and in both, accepted, loved, and honored for its raw reality. But I always am left with a feeling when she goes, wondering if I will ever see her again. But what can I do? I can only let her go and hope that she returns of her own will. Begging her would be a level of neediness that she would not respect. It would be this stickiness that she probably fears as well. And truth be told, I truly do not <u>need</u> her. Luckily, the foundation of peace that my soul has often rested upon has been intensely solidified in recent weeks. And throughout this roller coaster ride of a soul connection, I have been surprised to find that nothing really shakes me from my foundation too deeply. Things that I know that* *would have caused me impatience in the past can now barely even tap on the bubble of harmony that I feel within. Things that would have destroyed me emotionally, or things that would have annoyed me, or frustrated me, now all seem like the tickling of a feather in comparison to past reactive tendencies. And though this peace still resides, it's accompanied by a heavy heart. I truly yearned for what might possibly be a soul journey, with a soul that sees me at heretofore unknown levels. A soul for which to share the adventures of life, inward and outward, lifting each other higher, combining our insights and love; with a tender heart, two becoming one on the great pathway. I never believed in the romantic notion of "you complete me." I've always known that we have everything to complete oneself within each of us. But now that I've met a truly compatible soul, I can see how magical, beautiful, and more rapidly enlightening it could be to open all parts of one's being to another, to love, honor, and cherish one another while helping to expose new layers of understanding and perspective on the unlimited facets of existence through a shared vision. I can envision and feel the possibility of this melting together of our combination of frequencies, colors, and approaches to life that truly do seem to make each one more whole. This unique opportunity to find one that truly feels as an equal half now seems to be slipping away. And a pain dances on the surface of my foundation, sometimes quite loudly. It's a pain borne of the desire to love, to truly love at depths that I may have never known. But even though there's pain, there's an aroma of beauty in it. And I see that even pain doesn't have to be painful. It's just a word, a label that we give to a feeling. But if I dive deeper to the core of this feeling that I have now, there is still the ever present frequency of love. And no matter what happens in life, there is some teaching to be revealed. I shall not cover the pain. I shall embrace it. I shall embrace her in the infinite where we always meet, and carry on, knowing that my foundation is intact. And I'll await the next lessons that destiny deems fit for this ever expanding spark of life.*

Poem by son:

<u>Pain</u>

Somewhere in the pain
Lies a deeper call
Do not refrain
From letting yourself fall
Into a depth
Far beyond the above
In endless breadth
A cavern of love

31

Mother:

Ah, dear son... what an amazing unfolding has taken place. My heart aches as I know and feel your heart hurting. These are those unbelievable moments where life grabs us at the deepest level and somehow we have no choice but to go deeper and deeper. At the time of pain, we do not recognize yet that it hides a treasure... this is so logical - we would not call it "pain" if we knew. Our ignorance, our innocence, is the foundation for grandeur that comes undoubtedly next. The feeling of it has to be real before it can take fruition, and with this said... I searched back for a poem that I once wrote, when I had gone through some uncertain times as well with the one walking beside me. So in response to you, I give you this:

The Heart Break

*And so I call this the heart break...
Is that true, I wonder?
Abandoned I feel, misunderstood,
painfully hurt,
the challenge of loneliness
overshadowing me.
From all corners, I can see how fear
is masquerading itself in various forms
with deeply disturbing expressions*

to sway me into the waves of sadness,
negativity, despair.
Am I to continue on this path or
can I see that the loss of his loving eyes upon me
are showing me another way
to deepen the path towards my own eyes..?
The eyes of my own Soul...
they do not judge me,
they do not accuse me,
they do not frighten me...
Ah... they are so gentle,
so very tender,
so embracing all that I am.
And when I look deeply, I find that
his eyes have merged
into the eyes of my Soul,
and yes,
there they sparkle and love me unconditionally,
and this awareness allows me to embrace him
once again fully,
and this inner embrace heals not
only my suffering,
but his as well...
and so through the love, through the heart break,
the love and the heartbreak...
our path of struggles clears the way
for true unity
and harmony of our souls...
forever together...
and the Heart was never broken.

OK-ness

Mother:

    It is a rainy, cloudy, windy day today... I have to go to the store – but that is ok. As I am getting ready to go out the door, my shawl gets stuck on a door handle and I feel like letting out a small "curse" word... yet, I change that and say to myself "it's ok... you will be fine." I truly wonder how many times in a day that I say... "it's ok"... either to myself or to another. It turns out that it is a lot! Wow... what an interesting habit that is! Somehow, it must have a certain real intention and meaning. I remember when I was still a teenager in Holland, there was a book that did the rounds between many of us. Much of the contents I have forgotten, but I do know that it had quite an impact on many of my friends. It was called: "I am OK, You are OK." I had wonderful discussions with others about this topic at the time. Over the years, I have truly come to appreciate this marvelous short acknowledgment of life as it is. I love shortcuts... who does not?

And so, as always, when I come upon a new topic to explore, I start to play with it. I notice that saying it to myself seems to serve as an immediate attempt to feel better... is that really working or am I just covering up some unfriendly feelings inside of me? Is it an escape and I stubbornly keep at whatever the moment asks from me – so I don't need to delve deeper into my own issues? With this observation, I actually discovered another side of "ok." This one has nothing to do with the circumstances or happenings on the outer scale. This one pertains to my inner state. It has become a lovely discovery, and one that has allowed me to be more real with myself. At those very uncomfortable moments in life when I am completely and utterly incapable of feeling good inside, in actuality somewhat "pissed" off, seemingly at somebody, or some experience occurring at that moment... I have found that when I say to myself... "it is ok to feel that way," something happens. It is like a soothing balm. I am taking a step back, disengaged from my inner turmoil, and let go of the "angst," the anxiety to control myself inwardly. And this offers me a lovely opening of embracing the discomfort. And then I can see and feel more clearly the totality of my being where discomfort, pain, tears, and agony are accepted and allowed. It is OK... and I love this supremely handy "shortcut!" I also see it as genuinely helpful when talking to others who are experiencing anxiety, etc. It has the same effect. It has a gentleness about it. In actuality, it is a beautiful form of acceptance. No words or explanations are necessary... just a heartfelt "it's ok"... can soften anybody's heart. Not the "ok" with the circumstance, but the "ok" with the negative feelings. It is so much nicer than saying to somebody who is grieving, "just accept it"... that has become such a dry and almost rude approach. You might as well say... "get over it!" A gentle... "you are ok... it is all ok..." leaves a beautiful shared opening of humanness. I love the totality of the OK. Everything is OK, even when it is not OK, and I am OK with that.

Son:

What a great subject! I love it and it again demonstrates your playfulness with life. The first thing that this subject reminded me of, actually, was Australia. I have always distinctly and fondly recollected the way in which the Australian people respond to "thank you." It isn't the customary "you're welcome" that we are used to hearing here in the good ol' US of A. They respond with (cue Aussie accent) "no worries" or "no worries mate." Everywhere that you go, whether it be a 7-11 or a pub, "thank you" is, from what I saw, always responded to with "no worries." What an utterly lovely thing to hear all day, every day. I wish this was the case here. "You're welcome" is ok, I suppose. But hearing "no worries" directly or indirectly upwards of 50-plus odd times per day seemed to have some kind of effect. Almost like a mantra being repeated in your head. "No worries, no worries, no worries." It's very much like this OK-ness that you describe. I found the Australian people to be generally quite pleasant, and I thoroughly enjoyed my time there. It was certainly helped along by the lovely tune of worrilessness echoing through the air. And this mantric response to probably the most commonly spoken two words is something that always stuck with me. Even to this day (10 years later), there are times when I'll say this "no worries" to myself in my head (and always with an Aussie accent). There are times while cooking that I might spill the entire pan on the floor, or accidentally tip over my plate, ruining a good half hour-plus of preparation. Hard not to let out a barrage of verbal obscenities at any and all spirits or Gods that might be listening. But at times, I've caught myself, said "no worries mate," and simply did what needed to be done, which was to eat the food off the floor! Haha! Joking. But yes, even in moments like this, realizing that anger and frustration won't stop what has already happened, finding a place of OK-ness with it, and doing the next logical thing, is a great way to play with these otherwise unseemly events. We can choose how to react to any given situation. It feels good to let out a burst of frustration every now and again. But often, it feels even better to not worry about it, be ok with it, and continue on as if it was just another occurrence rising out of the substratum of all experiential happenings. And if you find yourself having what might be considered to be an overreaction, there's just another opportunity to say "no worries." We are human. We conditionally react. It's in our nature. It's ok to be ok with not having been ok. Through our awareness of how we act and react, we already begin to help along the upgrading and updating of human nature to one that is less reactive and more harmonic with the world around us. But honestly, either way, no worries mate!

Past

Mother:

The past... what to say about it..? That is a good question. I have found it to be quite a phenomenon. It comes to me at times as a thing of weight. And weight gives it its facade of importance, but yet, seemingly, I can clearly live without it. During most of the days, it is never felt nor thought about. But by golly... it is a sneaky thing, because truly it shows up everywhere. Seemingly weightless, it creeps into my daily life. It is an infiltrating object, a penetrating, obnoxious, persistent entity. Yep... now that I am writing about it – that is what it feels like: an entity. A faceless image, but with her tentacles touching everything, coloring it with her stubborn substance. I don't feel, for instance, last year or the year before, or the year before that. But the mirror tells me such a different story, that *unfortunately, I have to believe that she, the past... is somewhat of a real thing. Uggh... how annoying. I can't grab her and tell her to go away... nope, she sticks around and makes herself known in a thousand ways. The phone rings and I hear a familiar voice, and yes, there she is... she is reminding me of everything that this person has said to me, done to me, what I thought of her last week, last month, last year.., etc., etc., etc. And then here comes any kind of "work" that I need to do, and she (the Past), has engrained her stamps on everything that I perform. A thousand thoughts running through my head, how I should be doing it better..! Better would not exist if "she" (the Past) wasn't here! I find this an amazing scenario... her cloak covers everything. At closer look, I see that this is unavoidable. And so there has to be a good reason for her existence... nothing is created for nothing, I believe. I decide to have a more gentle approach to her and look for the advantages of her domineering nature. Ah, yes, of course, she also has a teaching in it for me. She reminds me of the pains of the yesterdays, the joys of times gone by, and allows me to see the whole kaleidoscope of stacked up feelings and emotions. As I now dress her up in a lightweight image of a butterfly, I detect a playfulness, and with that, my restrained reaction gives way to the open acceptance of the great potentials that she is actually indicating to me. Instead of rebelling against the remembrance of negative feelings, I see the chance to leave aside the fear of those repeated emotions and openly invite in the brightness of this new moment... aha... this is her true teaching: I can choose anew... I can embrace the one that I have talked to many times, but now see her as a new and fresh person, who also is different from yesterday... and I can embrace the image in the mirror, which is different from yesterday, but totally new today.*

The Past metamorphisized from the dense weight clinging onto me, into the light weight of a sweet reminder that I have choices...

I like it... she is welcome.

Son:

Past

What can I say about the past?
I can say that it has passed.
Sometimes slow, sometimes fast.
How much of it can I actually recall?
Just a tiny fraction, hardly anything at all.
Just moments or events at extremes of emotion,
Like waves or eddies on life's great ocean.
The peaks and valleys of joy or sorrow,
Everything in between, forgotten tomorrow.
There are many things that I miss about
being a child.

From my mother's daily kiss, to my sister's familiar smile.
In a way, it feels like a more real time.
Fully engrossed in play, more vivid was the mind.
When things hurt, they would hurt much more.
A tender heart exposed to feelings galore.
There was a fullness to this family life,
That now gives me longing for children and wife.
Reliving this past, alas, it has gone.
Who knows what will last, or be the morrow's dawn.
We want to hold on to what has no handle.
But it lives on like the glow of a burnt out candle.
Time is like a row of endless screens,
We can look in any direction, and choose the scene.
No matter where we choose to focus,
There is something here that we don't always notice.
There is this place where all time, memories, and connections converge.
Always the same face, infinite discoveries, and reflections to purge.
When I meet you there, more real than anything I've known.
Stillness in the air, far beyond what can be shown.
Though memory has its jars of nectar to taste.
This fire of loving presence lays it all to waste.
I wish this for every human to know,

This place of love, this place of flow.
How do we actually set to track
A place that we never truly lack?
Is it a touch of grace, or should we be fearless,
To reveal this place, that we deem so precious?
Maybe it's both, I don't really know.
I simply just asked, and it started to show.
Once you get a taste, it would be silly to go back.
That would be a waste, reliving patterns of past.
Love eternal awaits every soul.
Surrender to its call, be made whole.
Asking for help, don't worry, it's
really ok
Sometimes we need a loving hand to show us
the way.
This hand of which I speak, is
metaphorical indeed.
It reaches from everywhere, when we
seek in need.
Do not fear to look weak, or from
the eyes bleed,
For it is the humble and meek, that are unchained
and freed.
Be free, be free at last,
Nothing can harm one untethered from past.

Inspiration

Mother:

That is a brilliant word. I really like it because it refreshes my feelings with the promise of an opening. Not only an opening, but a fullness as well. I found myself telling my friend, with whom I share our daily "gratitude" list, that I am grateful for the inspiration to live well in all aspects of life. It immediately lifts me up to feel that. It creates a golden flow. What I like most about it, is the fact that it remains "anonymous." It doesn't give me any tangible promised outcome, something I will now have to look for and imagine what it could be, and how it will come. If that was the case, there would be the immediate potential for disappointment. And by golly, how I hate that word. I have, like all of you, these memories of the clearest moments in my life. And the one that I am going to tell you about is

44

one of those and it is truly a bit silly, but the simple fact is that the feeling that I had at that moment has been imprinted on my being. It was a long, long time ago in the early 70's. I remember entering the office of the head nurse of the hospital where I was working. It was in my native Holland. I had come to say goodbye to her since I was about to embark on my huge new life to the US, an enormous step in those years. She was very sweet. I had always liked her a lot. She asked some brief questions about my plans. And I burst forth with all the excitement in the world about the grand joy that I felt about my upcoming adventure. She remained silent for a moment, and then twisted her head gently to one side, and said: "I am just very worried about your enthusiasm, because it could be a big disappointment." Suddenly, I felt like I was transported to another planet, and I realized that on this planet Earth, there was such a thing as disappointments. It truly had never ever entered my mind. I was in shock that she could think such a thing. Fortunately, her concern never entered my being, and I inwardly shook my head about such a doubting attitude. Quite amazing that this moment has remained vividly in my mind... I can still feel that feeling and how it made me rise above such restrictive imaginations. It actually gave me more confidence, and I went hopping and skipping out the door. On I went to pack my stuff, and went off to the West Coast of the USA. And... I have never been disappointed! This, to me, sort of sums up how I see, feel, and hear "inspiration"... the knowing of the not knowing and yet totally knowing that this is so. Hopefully I do not sound too confusing! You see here it happened also... I felt inspired to the topic of inspiration, and although I had also played with the thought to one day write about my experience of the "disappointment" moment, the road has simply opened and now the link was made and both fit together.

Inspiration, I find, is a grand thing. Many times, we think about it only on the greater scale of doing big things: starting a new career, creating a symphony, or the likes, maybe becoming an actor, or whatever we imagine is bigger than we are now. But no... I found out that if I take it totally generic, it is applicable to everything. And if I use it like that - I leave behind the anxiety of the perfect outcome and don't weigh my life against such an imaginary scale. I simply feel, i.e., the inspiration to cook, the inspiration to go to the store, the inspiration to take a walk, the inspiration to smile at a passerby, or the inspiration to smile at myself. Yes, I am very grateful for the free fall into Inspiration...

Son:

This story of yours gives me some insight into this inspiration that you speak of. And this insight is that inspiration, coupled with doubt, is not very inspiring. This, you undoubtedly (pun intended) felt from your nurse friend there. Doubt can be like a cold steel mallet crushing down upon the warm fertile seed of what might otherwise become the most exquisite rose bush of a life that one might have never known. Imagine if you had taken her doubt to heart, and never ventured beyond what were her comfort zones. The glorious journey that has been your life would have likely been far more bitter. Bitterness at oneself for having lived a life ruled by doubt, rather than faith in the inspiring direction of your heart's call. A life without inspiration is a life half lived. Even half of the half of the half...

Inspiration

The garden of possibilities becomes barren,
dearth, dry and desolate
When we block her whispers from the
flourishing infinite.
The mind it is that seeks to know,
Which road to take, which way to go.
But it is only in the inspired unknown,
That the highest path is lit and shown.

I can remember times in my days gone by
That I felt her call, and questioned why.
If I follow this course that makes my
heart feel full,
Surely it will fail, and I'll look an
utter fool.
The more I fought, the more that I pondered,
The more I was distraught, sullen, despondent.
A heavy weight, like a sack of stones
A burden great, felt in my bones.
When I worried not whether I'd look insane,
A peace would gather, ignited like flames.
Inspiration is akin to a siren's call,
Follow it within, and in love you'll fall.
Knowing now that I knew nothing at all,
Of where true joy lies, not in mind small.
We have choices, every second, every day,
Which voices, beckoned, shall we obey?
The doubting and the questioning brain,
Blocks the way, leading to pain.
Pain is there to help us remember,
That true guidance lies in loving surrender.
Are we proud enough to think…. that we might
know better,
Than the One, who with a blink, created light,
and matter?
You may choose and you may stray,
You are free to put the compass away.
One thing that is certainly good to know,
Is that whatever steps taken, you always grow.

One way fast, one way slow,
The call never fades, you're never alone,
Throughout all your days, still always home.
We can never fail to arrive...
at the destination,
But much sweeter it is when alive...
with inspiration.
How to feel it, how to trust?
Just do it, try it, you really must.
With each fraction of a pace in faith you try,
You will be faced with a question of..."oh why?"
Why didn't I try, try this sooner,
To heed the song of the greatest crooner?
It soothes every ounce of my weary core,
Giving strength to try it once more.
With each new layer,
the resistance fading,
Through grace and prayer,
persistence upgrading.
Life comes now, with heretofore missing ease,
No longer such a chore, like a kissing breeze.
"I want to know what's next,"
says the mind notorious,
But the silent way, more direct,
gold lined, glorious.
It's just like the changing of a radio station,
Static between, then tuning in... to inspiration.

The Tides

Son:

After many days of feeling superb, today, suddenly, I do not. I thought not to write while being in this mood. But actually, why not? It's real; it's the way it goes sometimes. So, I call this...

The Tides

The tides, the ebb and flow
Rising and falling
Pushing and pulling
Through sun, rain, hail, or snow.
Up, down, around and again
Forces of the Earth, forces of the wind.
Who knows what happens,
What the next moment brings,
If a door closes or opens,
The bird is eaten or sings.

Such is life, beyond control,
Though with strife, and rigmarole,
We try to bend, mold and fold,
Try to upend heat, turned into cold.
We have successes, as well as failures
We have duresses, and also raptures.
What can we do but ride the train,
Holding an umbrella in a hurricane.
Just get wet, the choice is lost,
The hedged bet has too high a cost.
Either... or, descend or soar
Neither rich, neither poor,
Lie in a bed, lie on the floor,
Clear your head, or think some more,
Do something, do nothing, feeling bored,
Is there anything that I can do to be adored?
Should I go, or should I stay?
Maybe I'll grow, perhaps decay.
Can I find peace in these changing tides?
Perhaps in the East, perhaps in the skies?
It's not always so simple to just be,
Difficult at times to relax and see.
Am I doing it right, am I doing it wrong?
Day turns to night, ofttimes for far too long.
I had it, then I lost it, has it escaped?
I'm glad, then sad, empty thoughts with weight.
At times alone, at times whole,
Whatever shown, good for soul.
I tire, I exhaust, I energize, and awaken,
Through fire and frost, stabilized, then shaken.

Life is like a box of chocolates,
Hard as rocks or quite the delicates.
The flavor sweet, possibly salty,
Maybe a treat, or heavy and hearty.
What goes up, must come down,
You can smile, you can frown,
Fill the cup, but don't drown,
Be a devil, be a clown.
Do you have fatigue from this ferry ride?
Or more intrigue from every side?
One thing is for sure, behind the great curtain,
Is something endlessly pure, and forever certain.
The tides are sure to ebb and flow,
But peace is there, I hope you know.

Mother:

I love your poetry. Such richness. A wonderful avalanche of flowing words expressing from all angles the madness of the Tides. And truly that is what it is to me: sheer madness! A roller coaster ride of soul stirring ups and bizarre downs. As a woman, I have, of course, had quite a hay day with this. Our menstrual cycle gives us that physical excuse to battle with those moments. I do believe that because of that natural occurrence, we are quite well prepared for these unpleasant waves. Having said that, there's no doubt that I relate vividly to your description of the Tides in the realm of our spiritual well-being.

By golly... such unexpected turns it takes, and meanwhile, one has to learn to breathe through it. It is almost like childbirth... we are supposed to take deep breaths and not think during those births. I have to admit that I am far from being gracious with this! Whenever I am in utter darkness, I immediately allow myself to fall into despair and not try to fix it, and I always cry!! Yep - I am a woman and I love to cry, my helplessness flows over into the warm teardrops streaming freely down my flustered cheeks. Somehow, it relaxes me, and makes me acknowledge that, yes, I am in a pit! And so we swing like the pendulum. Looking back at these ups and downs, I can tell you that when I am deaf from hearing the celestial silence, I console myself after the crying fit, with the certainty that the "up" is on its way, just around the corner..! I can breathe... I shall wait... and when the sky is clear... well, ha... then it gets funny, because I feel so pristinely complete, that any thought of a "fall" doesn't enter my being. The glory of that state makes me immune to negativity. In other words, looking back at my ups and downs, the positive sense of life has been predominant during my earthly years so far.

Once I read your words on Tides, I immediately thought back to a moment of deep darkness in which I wrote a poem. I will copy it below and follow it up with one of those poems from my moments of great delight! This will undoubtedly bring to the foreground how these Tides are occurring in my life. For sure, it will perfectly depict my extremes!

The dark moment made me write the following, and since the darkness was complete, no title came to mind, and therefore, the title remained exactly that:

NO TITLE

Total sadness reigns in my heart, mind and soul...
how did it get so deep...
so mysteriously deep...
so without answers,
so without any label other than sadness.
Any attempt to find clarity becomes numb
in its effort.
Lost, mute and deaf, it has announced itself,
and here it is...
and somehow, here I am also...
or just a reflection of me,
I no longer know..?
Courage has faded away...
sense and sensibility have deluded me...
My page is not long enough
for the question marks...
tired of writing them...
I blankly drop it all...
In the void I remain,

in the vacuum I sit...
better not to catch thoughts,
better not to examine feelings,
better not to analyze emotions...
I have none...
and so I sit,
I sit and let it be...

And here is the one I wrote while basking in the Up-Moment:

<u>PERFECT DAY</u>

How sweet it is... today all is clear,
clouds have evaporated,
soft peace is resounding,
the flow of perfection revealed.
The inner being endlessly expanding,
borderlessly embracing all...
Silence sings loudly through my veins
and into the ether...
its echo reverberating throughout my being
and throughout the seeming universe.
No density - no weight - no pulls
Only light - only giving - only joy - only Love
This is my day and
it is perfect.

Such opposites... and yet both seem natural. I actually believe that somehow we have become accustomed to this and have learned to simply enjoy the movement of the swaying! It is truly the Pendulum of Life. I can see us being two children on the playground, and having a fun time being on the swings - taking in the sweet flowing of the motion, and as we pass each other in the air, we smile, laugh and giggle from joy. We are playing the Game of Life and the Game of Life is playing us... and all is well.

Grace

Son:

What is grace? Is it something that we deserve, or through actions, earn? Is it only available to a lucky few that seem to have divine favor while the rest are shunned? Where does it come from and how do we know that it exists? I don't know how to answer that. I only know that grace is guiding me to write about grace.

Sitting here, trying to find what to say, it feels as though an opening has entered into my space. Everything feels somewhat spatial. My body feels lighter, and my heart feels calm as if soaked in aromatic, bubbly bath water. It's warm, it's soothing, everything feels softer. I hear the ever-present buzzing of sound as it vibrates through my current state of vivid awareness. Is it the electricity, the sockets, the TV, the fridge? I'm not sure. None of them are on or running. It's a *good thing that my fridge is not running. If my icebox starts sprinting around, that might actually freak me out and cause a real existential crisis. Haha! But seriously, everything is off, the fridge motor is silent, but yet this buzzing persists. But it's familiar, not annoying. If I go into the middle of nowhere, at this level of opened, awakened attention, will I still hear the vibrating hum of existence? I'm thinking probably yes. But the middle of nowhere is nowhere near my present here, so I'm sorry, I can't give immediate feedback on that query. But I feel like I've noticed this cosmic murmur in nowhere-land before. I believe that everything vibrates with some form of rhythmic constancy. Is this the Om? Is it the remnants of the Great Word from which all of creation emerged? This is getting deep, but never mind, I just discovered a gnat buzzing in my ear! That's it! I think he was just trying to talk to me about this chapter. He wants it to be about fruit. How graceful fruit is! Ha! But actually, maybe that's not a bad segue, little flying buddy. Fruit is quite the gracious miracle. A display, if you will, of grace in physical manifestation. How can soil, water, and sun alone produce such a complexity and variety of flavors, aromas, textures, colors, and nutrients? How can it be? Take the heavy, dense, alligator skinned avocado, for example. So full of healthy fats, minerals, and creamy goodness. How did the avocado tree get fat into its fruits? Is there fat in the dirt? Did it rain bacon grease while I was sleeping? I don't understand how it can be? For contrast, take the light, sweet, juicy strawberry. Nature's natural dessert! Same dirt, same water, same sun. Did somebody dump a bunch of sugar on the ground by the berry bush? How did it get so succulently sweet, delicately and deliciously flavored, all while tickling my delighted fingers with its seedy, but subtle exterior? It even comes with a cute little green hat for which to hold it by, while you gleefully ingest this treasure from the Earth. The strawberry red is the most beautiful hue of red that I've ever seen. Against the contrast of its green top, it simply must be grace in fruity form. Put it on the canvass of a cloud of white whipped cream, and the heavens will be jealous. First thing that comes to mind: Never write while hungry! Second: I think the gnat is on my shoulder now crying tears of love! But truly, the miracle of nature, if pondered, is one of undeniable, ceaseless grace.*

For some reason, this topic of grace is taking me in another direction entirely. Maybe because I just ate a bowl of strawberries! Thinking of grace, I'm reminded of some years that I spent in India. I can distinctly recall playing the sport, cricket, with the local adults and kids from the surrounding villages. I saw that they often wore the same clothes each day and rarely had shoes. Frequently, they were... how shall I say, not devoid of dirt on their clothing or persons. Hair was quite unkempt. But they always seemed happy. They were carefree in nature, enjoying whatever they had, even if it wasn't much. I would walk by the areas where they lived and see their parents and grandparents, likewise, in paltry circumstance. However, often they were with great big smiles, gathered around some makeshift outdoor table, having talks, enjoying a steaming cup of hot chai. Where they lived, by our standards, you wouldn't necessarily even define it as a home. The entire dwelling might be the size of a single car garage, sometimes less. No running water (buckets from a local well), the toilet is a hole outside, and if lucky, maybe some electricity. Heaven forbid if it rained! The roofs were a patchwork of whatever shelter looking objects that could be hobbled together. But they didn't sit around and bemoan their lot in life. They joked, they laughed, they stuck together, smiled, and had a lightness about whatever they could find to be joyous about. Is that grace? To have an inner lightheartedness, regardless of worldly possessions? Or is it grace to have external abundance, while being depressed? I think I'd prefer to have a good attitude towards life throughout any and all possible situations, rather than living in external plenty, but with internal poverty. Of course, grace to have both internal and external riches seems ideal. Some do have this. And bless them for balancing the two, for it certainly is a potential outcome of giving a man of internal riches, some external wealth, that he then loses the richness of spirit. Often, what we want may not be where the greatest lessons manifest for our souls. So perhaps, the greatest trick is to find grace in whatever it is that may come our way. Not to judge whether we like it or not. But to accept that there must be a lesson in it, and once understood, might open us up to lighter, gentler lessons that aren't as rough around the edges, far less burdensome, and easier to learn as our resistance to grace eases.

This will be a long chapter as I will try to illustrate from my own life how different situations can be dealt with in a softer way than might be considered normal. But it goes into displaying grace in a more all-encompassing way, which I find pertinent and useful in the context of seeing what grace can mean, redefined.

First example would be when I first moved to NYC in my mid-20's. Ironically, during my first night in NYC, somebody broke into my car, and stole everything from the trunk, even though nothing was visible from the outside. Welcome to NY! I'd say there was about $5,000 worth of various items in there. Maybe it was a sign of things to come. Anyways, I had saved up some money before heading to the Big Apple so that I *had time to look for work, get a place to live, etc. I don't remember exactly how many months went by as I tried to find work, but nothing was coming my way. I eventually got to a point where I had spent all my money, maxed out my credit cards, rent was due in 2 weeks, and I had $5 in my wallet. Literally, my bank account was at $0 and not even $1 of credit remained. My family, as lovely as they are, was never blessed with material wealth. So, conveying my dire situation to them would not have achieved any purpose, other than to make me heavyhearted at the thought of their concern for me. Also, the idea of returning to live with them again didn't feel right to me. I was somewhat surprised at how calm I was in this situation. I remember, during my inner conversations with the One, saying "Ok, Lord, if this is what you want for me, who am I to think that I know better? If there is some lesson for my soul to be gleaned from being homeless, then I accept it. Maybe you want me to experience life in a homeless shelter. Maybe I can be of some service there, perhaps comforting the downtrodden with an open heart, attentive ear, or kind words. Perhaps that is part of my journey at this time, and my soul will be grateful for the lessons found there." For the most part, I truly felt quite accepting of my potential financial and worldly impending doom. With the last $5 in my pocket, I made my way to the local internet cafe.*

Same as I had done countless times before. I didn't own a computer, so this was my place to check emails, look for jobs, read about strawberries, etc. This was also in the days before our phones became capable of all these things. So, there I sat, sending out resumes and work requests for anything that I was capable of doing. I did this for the full time allotment that my $5 would buy me. When that time was up, I stood and thought, "This is it. This is my final straw. I have nothing left. I have food for a few more days. My roommate is unaware that he might not get my share of the rent coming up. But I accept whatever is next." As I stepped out of the internet cafe, directly outside, on the sidewalk, was a $50 bill! Nobody around! I immediately felt a lightness in my heart. I somehow knew that everything would be ok. I felt as if I had crossed some threshold, almost like a test. Not that I would say that God tested me. But it was a good test anyways for me, to know how I would handle such a situation. Sometimes you never know until you pass through it. It's one thing to say how you would be and an entirely different thing to actually experience your inner state under such perceived calamity. Even though I say that I felt everything would be ok, that doesn't mean that I had expectations of getting a job. Just knowing that I could buy another week's worth of food already gave me the sense that I was somehow *being taken care of. It gave me a deeper sense of calm. The finding of that money let me know that for whatever path that I was headed, it was safe, so long as I continued to trust. So long as I continued to find and believe that grace was coming in all forms, regardless of normalized conceptions of what grace might or should look like. I knew that I wouldn't starve and die. That never entered my mind. But, lo and behold, after months of failure, on the next day, I got a call for a job! It was a bartending job. I was working a couple days later, immediately started stacking up tips, and just had enough for rent exactly when it was due! Just in the nick of time! Homelessness wasn't in my cards after all!*

I have one more story for this reforming of the definition of grace. After bartending, I ended up in the wild world of catering. In many ways, it was quite enjoyable. We worked for some of the most rich and famous people in the world. From the Dalai Lama, Wall Street elite, politicians, kings, queens, to fashion shows, crazy parties, weddings, museum events, and any other possible reason for people to gather. We did it all. There was certainly no monotony to the work. Every day was something new, some grand new house, or spectacular apartment overlooking Central Park, interesting guests, overhearing inside information on things that the "street folk" may never get to hear. It was exciting. I was fortunate enough to *meet the right people to get aligned with some of the best in the business. I also worked with some of the most lovely people that I've ever had the pleasure to know. It was quite a blessing. Of course, as with anything, the job had its caveats. Some clients could be unnecessarily cruel or demeaning due to their self-perceived higher worldly stature. Not all, but some. Some events were excruciatingly long. I kid you not; I once was part of a VIP wedding, where I did not even have a chance to sit down for 27 hours! I only got to grab bites of food at random while in pursuit of my next task. Many days, I worked two or three events. I'd do a morning event, afternoon, and evening event as well. I very often worked 12+ hours per day, 6 or 7 days a week. I would even go the gym many nights at 2 or 3am after getting home, then sleep a few hours and do it all over again. I had a hard time saying no to any work. Perhaps I didn't want to disappoint the company that was requesting my service, choosing me from a pool of available and qualified prospects. I figured the more that I said yes to any and all requests, the higher up I'd move in their minds of being reliable, willing, and able to be a constant and irreplaceable part of a team. And it worked. I even got to the point of leading or "captaining" events. And I made a lot of money. A lot for me anyways. I'd say that I often made $6-10,000 per month. This was my normal for quite a few years.*

Besides the hours, and the few ornery clients, there were other parts of the work that were no walk in the park either. Often, these events were outdoors (i.e. weddings). When it's 90-100 degrees outside with near 100% humidity, and you have to carry tables, chairs (don't get me started on bagging at times hundreds of chairs... yes putting each chair in a bag!), carrying case after unending case of alcohol and every other beverage known to man, bins of plates, bins of utensils, ovens, glassware, decorations, and more, all while nobly bedecked in a tuxedo, across literal hill and dale, fields o' plenty, and sweating more than a camel can drink in a week; I daresay that even the finest of athletes would reach peak exhaustion after 12-18 hours under such conditions and physical demand. It's only important to know about this to understand the future weight of the coming tragedy. After years of working at this, perhaps insane, extreme level, I was able to pay off all debts, and start saving. Once I started to surpass $20K in savings, I began to evaluate what options there might be for investment. There was a prior negative experience with stock investing that became worthless overnight due to bankruptcy. Because of this, I didn't trust holding any stock overnight. Especially since in that particular case, the financial statements of the company turned out to be mostly fabricated lies. On paper, they looked *great, and the prospects for growth were huge. They were signing deals with big box retailers in the relatively new market of budget LCD TV's at that time, and I saw their commercials on TV. Everything looked locked and loaded, couldn't go wrong. Turns out that they mostly invented the numbers, stole the investors money, went belly up, and skipped the country. And the SEC couldn't do anything about it. There were court hearings, but those that were ultimately responsible were long gone.*

I digress, that's another story. But it was hard to invest after that, not knowing, and having no guarantee that the financial statements of a company were actually truthful. If companies could print whatever they wanted and rob us blind, I wasn't going to try that again. So, I figured that it was safer to day trade. You get in and out of trades in less than 30 minutes. Impossible to lose everything. If it looks bad, you just get out with some loss, but not total loss. No risk of holding a stock overnight while a company implodes during your slumber, awakening to a real life bad dream. After deciding to focus on day trading, I spent a year reading multiple day trading books, taking online courses, watching video after video, and doing practice trades on demo accounts until I felt confident enough to put real assets on the line. By the time that I figured out which strategies that I liked, I discovered a trading robot that you could lease the rights to use. You could utilize this robot software to backtest strategies to see how they performed against past technical data. You could actually see how much money you would have made or lost, for example, in the past 6 months or more based on the triggers and parameters that you set in the robot. What a great tool! I tweaked and adjusted the virtually unlimited combination of parameters until I squeezed every dime of potential success out of my strategy. Then I started using it to scan markets and place trades in real time on my behalf. This was great, as it removed emotions like fear, adrenaline, and excitement from the equation. Just pure technical execution, done with precision. And it worked! I didn't make money every day, but I made money most days. Each day, the robot would find between 1-10 trades per day. Sometimes more, but rarely more than 10. The days that I made money were also of higher dollar amounts than my loss days. I'd say I made money two out of every three days on average. As long as the profits on good days were of greater significance than the loss days, that's a huge success. Most weeks, I came out ahead. Probably around 90% of the time. When I started day trading, I began with $25K in capital. This is the minimum required by law to be able to be considered a pattern day trader. I had reached over $40K in *capital some months later. But there was an anomalous day to come, something that I had no plan for. There was a day that, at the time, was the single largest intraday fall of the stock market in history. I had no plan for it, because it had never happened before. I could have protected myself by placing a limit on the amount of trades that the system could place in a day. I did not use that feature because I wanted as many trades as possible, knowing that long term, the strategy came out ahead. So, the more the better. And it was rare to find more than 10 hits anyways. What I did not calculate or anticipate, since it had never happened before, was that there could be a situation where almost every stock in the market would hit my triggers. But that fateful day, it happened. My system triggered thousands of buy signals. I was at work while all this was happening automatically on my computer at home. I was powerless to do anything about it. Now, this occurrence would have been ok, great actually, if all the money used in those purchases was my own money. But I was using a margin account, whereby the bank would loan me 4 to 1 on my money. So my $40K became $200K of available funds to trade. Banks do this to encourage trading at higher volumes. More profit for them also. There's also almost no risk of losing such an amount when day trading, because you'd be out of a trade long before it got* *anywhere even near 1% loss of your own starting capital. The only issue with trading with the banks money is that they can force you to sell out of a position before you want to if they have any trepidation about potential losses of their capital. And that is exactly what the bank did, literally wiping out my entire life savings in an instant. All my years of blood, sweat, tears, studying, and saving. All the backbreaking, painstaking, tireless, determined hard work... POOF! Gone! Just like that. Back to square one. I did the math later on to see what would have happened if the banks would not have forced me out of all those trades. I would have made around $280,000 that day! The strategy would have worked if it was allowed to finish. Instead, I was wiped out. I couldn't trade any more.*

I think when the dust settled, I was able to withdraw just a few hundred dollars. That was all that was left. I did have a couple thousand in my checking account. But nowhere near the $25K that I would need to be able to continue trading. I was so confident in my strategy, that I kept most of my money in my trading account. I felt that the more that I had there, the more profit that I'd make, so why not?

In hindsight, a limit to the amount of trades would have been smart, or trading with only my money. Either of those things would have prevented that loss. But the moral of the story is *that I was ok. I used the proverbial "no worries mate," and put one foot in front of the other. What else could I do? I never screamed, never cried, didn't pull my hair out, and I slept like a baby. Sure, I was upset, disappointed; for having felt like all those grueling days of work and years of practically having no life, so that I could adhere to my insane work ethic, had just been for naught and erased. It wasn't as much about the money as it was about that. But regardless, I was quite surprised with myself, in a way, at how calmly I was able to just move past it. I went to work the next day, totally normal, told nobody of what had happened, and felt gratitude for having been young enough that it was not my life savings towards the end of my life when work wouldn't have been so easy to perform. It was another moment for me to surrender, and say "Clearly there must be some grace in this. The stock market has been a bit of a curse for me, it must not be my destiny. I have a job. No big deal." And I went on, hardly any worse for the wear. And who knows, if I would have made $280K that day and continued on to be a millionaire, I probably wouldn't have been who I am today. I wouldn't be sitting here writing these words. Who knows what would have happened? I might have crashed my private jet while trying to kill the gnat in my ear that was trying to buzz to me about its love for strawberries.*

This chapter is about grace. It was a long road, but bear with me. I think we need to redefine what grace looks, feels, and acts like. Every experience, every moment, every tragedy or windfall has an element of grace in it. There's always a reason, even though it might be impossible to see that while in the throes of darkness. Faith is not about believing that you'll get what you want. Faith is about believing that what you are experiencing and receiving is somehow what your soul needs to grow to its next level, and being ok with that. I've had some more even apparently worse "so called" tragic experiences in my life that I won't get into here. But no matter how "dark" or tragic the experience, I always try to find a lesson, something positive to take from it, and keep those as cornerstones to add to the foundation of my being. We can find something positive in ANY situation, no matter how shocking or horrid it might be labeled by the mind or society. We have that choice. We have that power. Victimhood is a choice. Let's decide to be strong, stand up, move forward, and find a positive lesson, no matter how small, from every experience. Let's choose that and we open ourselves to see grace everywhere, feel it pouring down upon us, and each moment becomes a moment of grace, of blessing, of love. Grace is natural. It is only thoughts and doubts that block the stream. We can relax, it's all ok, no worries, just wait, just see, inspiration will come, pain will wane, and grace shall imbue every speck of our reality. Grace consumes all because it is all.

Mother:

Grace, that fluid invisible mysterious force of Life, so evasive for the mind, yet permanently present in all and everything. Your description of how our Mother Earth manifests these miraculous gifts almost brings tears to my eyes. How incredibly beautiful Her grandeur is, and how fortunate we are to be aware of these wonders, and therefore tangibly connected with the all-pervading Grace that life bestows upon us... and then, yes... the not so obvious workings of grace start flopping us around on our "worldly journey." I think your theme for this chapter goes in perfect flow with our last chapter of "Tides!" It is oftentimes very helpful to look back and see how and what happened to us and notice that serene still string of peace weaving through all of it, and now we can say; "yes, it was grace."

Reading your accounts of those monstrous experiences makes me shiver on the one hand, and yet, to see how this made you grow, I, on the other hand, embrace the workings of grace in your life. Needless to say, I have had my own explosions of hidden grace, as you well know.

Too many to relate, but at this very moment, two of them stand out.

It was early spring of 1980. Once again we found ourselves without money, without jobs, etc., etc. We were invited to stay at the basement apartment of a friend of Dad's to see if our luck would turn, this time in Oregon. The four of us (Dad, your sister, you and I) drove from Colorado to Oregon. Once there, the car broke down, no luck at all with jobs, and soon our dire circumstances became too much for the friend. He was kind enough to let us borrow his pick-up truck and $1000, and we were sent on our way to mystery land. Never will I forget that morning that we left. It was quite early and the drizzly rain made visibility hard. The house was in the country, so we drove through foggy fields and hills over skimpy unpaved back roads. It truly felt like one of those dreary landscapes in sad movies. Two babies in diapers on the floorboard, (no child seats in those days) and about 20 cardboard boxes with our belongings in the back. We spoke little and drove southbound to San Francisco and took a cheap motel. Dad got the phone book out and called to look for jobs as soon as we got there. Everything seemed to close the door on him. He definitely got the sense that this was not the place to keep forcing the issue. "No," he said, "we need to go more south." And so we did. We packed our little family up, and the next morning, we left the motel and the busy franticness of the San Francisco traffic. First, south on the freeways, and then soon we made our way west. And then for me, one of the greatest moments of my life popped up..! We hit the coast... the 101 Highway... never before had I seen such indescribable beauty... my mind disappeared into its splendor, my heart burst open, a breathless bliss engulfed my whole being. This remained for quite some time. I had wings of gold and it was not until the intensity slowed down that I realized the insane contrast with my worldly circumstances. It made me laugh for the severity of these outer conditions was nowhere to be found. From that moment onward, there was not a single doubt about the good outcomes life had in store for us. And so it was... we drove down to Santa Maria, and there, Dad found a sales job immediately, which was to be a bit more south in Oxnard. He got a company car, a steady salary , and commissions on top of that. The next day, we found a sweet apartment half a block from my beloved Pacific Ocean and that is where Grace decided to bring us. And a glorious time we spent there..! You had just turned one year old, and on our first morning in Oxnard, you started to walk for the first time... ready to go on your own miraculous journey!

Another experience that comes to mind, maybe a bit less dramatic, took place much, much *later, somewhere in the early 2000's. As always, money in those days remained scarce. Through various circumstances, it always eluded us. Meanwhile, I had discovered a talent for painting and, lo and behold, I actually sold them regularly at a local farmers market. During this moment in time, I had delved into Byron Katie's book, "Loving What Is," with the four pertinent questions. I loved this book tremendously, and it obviously was a huge help in everyday life. And really, how comical it all becomes with her 4 questions. As a reminder, the first question: "are you sure?" Second one: "are you absolutely sure?" Third one: "how do you feel if you don't think that thought?" Fourth one: "is there any stress free reason to keep that thought?" Ha... that gets you on the right path immediately. And so it happened. Before going to the farmers market after our coffee and toast, I noticed that all we had left in the house for food was one can of pork and beans! Yep... that is right, not exactly health food stuff. I can still clearly picture that can sitting in my cupboard. I looked at it and thought, "wow, that is all we have left, this is not so good," and on top of that, the rent is due and we haven't even a penny. But immediately, Byron Katie's questions came to mind and I realized that I was totally fine without that thought. It made me laugh, and off we went. We got in the van, packed full with the tent, chairs, table, backboards, and paintings for the market and started down the road for our 30 minute drive. Halfway there, the van broke down! Luckily, it was nearby to the house of one of my friends, and they gracefully let us borrow their pickup truck. Quickly, we transferred the contents from van to truck and hurried to the market. To make a long story short, as soon as I started unpacking, people started buying all morning long, and we had enough money to pay the rent, buy nice groceries, and enough to fix the van! What wondrous happenings just to make me realize that I am taken care of.*

Amazing to look back at all of that. Your stories, my stories, these Tides of Life! The inner ones and the outer ones – how incredible to recognize that it was to bring us to greater inner fruition. It is easy to see that although we lived through these extreme events, what remains is not bitterness, but sweet joy..! That, to me, is the biggest proof that all and every part of it was Grace.

Intention

Mother:

Waking up this morning, I searched through the still somewhat misty forest of my thoughts. Eagerly trying to find a clearing that would bring me the longed for lighter version of this daybreak. It felt like I was playing hide and seek with what intent the day had for me. A hint – a soft calling... is it there? Where are you hiding? Can't you make yourself a little clearer... and so it went - until seemingly I stopped that roaming around in the haziness of waking up. I wanted to have a direction and that is when the thought came to me... I want to feel joy today. I want to feel light; I don't want the heaviness of somber thoughts. Do I need to diligently work on this, or will this longing be enough to manifest it, I wondered? Quite quickly, the imagined schedule of the day started to emerge. Ok... I said... that is all well and good, but if I jump into that program, will I remain with this lightness, or am I going to be a bit dragged down into a disciplinary sense of accomplishing something? Ah... such a crazy mixture of sweet questions. So far, it doesn't feel heavy yet... just a slight sense of maybe a winter coat calling to be put on..? But I don't want her... I gently eschew it, and now, after my cup of coffee, my senses are awake, and I feel more able to steer through the calling of a direction for today. And so it comes to me... is there an intent that the day is bringing forth in me, or is there the call for an intention on my part? What a sweet game to figure out! The intent feels more like a set goal to me, while the idea of intention leaves me a bit more space to put my own stamp on it. I decide to pay more attention to my intention than to the intent of the day. I love playing with this because, meanwhile, it truly makes me more aware of what is going on, not only on the outer level, but most of all, on the inner one. This is interesting: I noticed that when I zoom in more upon my intention of feeling light and ease, that the intent for the day with the regular schedule changed! I suddenly see an opening for a much bigger and brighter way to celebrate this day... and yes, now the word, "celebrate," emerges. I had no feeling whatsoever about celebrating this day when I first opened my sleepy eyes this morning. Since I really wanted to take the train of

ease, now this is changing everything. I am celebrating..! What am I celebrating... the light of the day... or the glory of the abundant beauty of nature around me? Am I celebrating the company that keeps me? Am I celebrating the lovely taste of coffee and my breakfast food? Ha... all I know for now is that I am definitely celebrating the intention that I set this morning!! As far as the intent that the day had for me... I have no idea, but somehow it truly feels that it was changed, but then again, that is only the side of the outer manifestation of the day. Most likely, the intent of the day was for me to find my true and genuine intention, and the two merged... the inner and the outer once again having engaged in their never ending game of finding the natural balance, where Life is celebrated in its totality...
I love setting intentions!!

Son:

As always, you engage in so many things with a playful nature. It's a really sweet way to go about life. I've always struggled with this word "intention." I've never been too sure of whether or not it's just desire in a fancier word dress. I've always felt that our highest good and most miracle laden way of living is to simply surrender to the inner guidance, the silent and gentle pushing in a given direction that becomes illuminated most easily through heart vibrating way signs that then become reflected and translated by the mind into the appropriate course of action. So, I've felt that by "intending" anything, there is a danger of closing off a brighter, more harmonious outcome from a space of no intentions.

That being said, at the same time, having experienced and felt at times that our true nature just so happens to be as a spark of the divine, then perhaps, why shouldn't we create? For us to breathe, or even have a heartbeat, we must have this spark of life at our core. It is this life force that moves all the heavens, earth, universe, energy, and matter. If we are this life force, then why not acknowledge it, accept that we are the One Life contained in a temporary shell, and use that sacred gift to co-create or intend our way to a more positive, loving, or peaceful existence through our focused perception of our unique angle on reality.

In actuality, I believe that it might be even more interesting to combine the two aforementioned approaches to living day by day. Maybe we can live in surrender and intention at the same time! In a way, I like the idea of intending. It's like a prayer. It is using a space of wishfulness within. Whether that be intending to be a better person, intending to achieve a goal that would give joy, praying for another human *spark of light to feel healthier or more whole, often the very act of intending, itself, comes from a genuine space of love. Loving oneself enough to intend something more positive, or loving others with likewise positive and loving vibes. It's sweet. It is playful. Perhaps, it's a natural flow of love from the Great Force. So, maybe in the act of surrendering to a higher will beyond our own, we can tap into this force, feel what it intends for us, and then actively, rather than passively, participate in that surrendered calling. That way, we humbly receive our guidance, and then use our given force of will to continue reverberating that intention throughout the cosmos. It sounds like an unstoppable combination of forces that can only have a positive outcome for any and all beings that intersect on this woven web of creative light strings. Light strings pulsing through creation from the eternal creative source, unblocked, supported within, and allowed free reign with its undying potential. This web that is woven through the surrendered heart and focused intent can have no other possible outcome than miracles. Miracles of osmosis, touching and transforming all other energetic forms of life into lighter, sweeter, more loved, and more free expressions of the One Life. The intention from guidance, and my intention as I write this, is for all to be the best versions of ourselves, to know that we are loved, to find peace, and to heal the world through the intentional purification of our inner states of being. I believe and I trust that, collectively, we all can transform our existence into paradise. I surrender and intend for this to be true. Be still and know love.*

Endurance

Mother:

"Lift it higher, no not enough, higher still. Come on, keep going," the teacher urged me on to elevate my leg higher, while sweat dripping off my body, trying to ignore the pain and accepting that this is the only way to do it. This is what took place many, many decades ago during my intense ballet hours. Never doubting that one has to work hard to get results, building and building ever more endurance. It seemed, now that I am looking back, as if it was the fashion of the times. I honestly start to wonder if it also has anything to do with my European upbringing. I remember the freezing cold days, lots of either rain, snow, or stiff winds, and nonetheless, the bicycles were taken out of the shed and mom waved us goodbye as we threw our heavy schoolbags on the bikes to prepare for the challenging trip to school. Mighty

cold those days were. And during lunch break, we made the same trip back home, then back to school again for the afternoon, and then finally being done at 4pm. Nowadays, these kinds of scenarios are unheard of. The most amazing part, when I think back, is that it was completely taken for granted. We didn't complain. We knew it had to be like that. And guess what... my mom would never say: "be careful" (and she loved us all dearly!). That sort of comment didn't exist. Nothing like "you poor thing." No, none of that. You simply did it like the rest of the family and it was accepted as part of life. Doing my ballet classes on top of that, with also not much compassion for our physical state of relaxation, the word endurance became imprinted in my mind. It is seemingly a thread that is seen as a necessary part of life, especially when I think about the incredible hard days of the life of my mother. She would get up before dawn to go to the shed to get the coal to take into the house to start the heater in the living room. Then, she would prepare breakfast for seven of us, and when it was all ready and nice and warm in the living room, she woke us up to come downstairs to eat our breakfast together before each of us went off to our various schools, etc. And that is not to mention how the rest of her day looked. You can well imagine with the cleaning of the house, the making of the beds, the preparing for lunch, dinners, and all the coffees or teas in between. And on specific days, there was a huge stack of laundry to be washed by hand. What else but endurance could save her days..! My own years as a mother were nothing like that, but at the same token, I feel that it did call forth in me a certain stance about endurance. The constant sense of alertness, truly day and night, making sure that the babies were alright, that they had everything needed, etc., etc. Somehow, time to think did not present itself very often. Is it a drive to perform well? Is it a drive, like a natural instinct for survival? Is it to push aside the necessary inward reflection, and using endurance as a sort of scapegoat?

As years go by, I do find myself saying more often: "I no longer want to muster up enough courage to endure this." Ha, wow, what a statement! Endurance failing? And then I wonder immediately if I have gotten perhaps weaker over the years and my inner energy is flustering away in the wind. Am I getting tired of living at those moments? Or maybe, just maybe, just very much maybe (don't worry, I will not continue this "maybe" mantra!), is life simply showing me that it is time for a change? It looks like one of the hardest things in my life has been to go easy on myself and relax. As I mentioned, from childhood on, there was simply no room given to "go easy." It felt more like there was a pattern of conduct given to each of us to fulfill without questions. This, in my case, has remained somehow embedded in my system. It was not until my later years that I started to recognize this, and first of all, I embraced that recognition, and accepted it as a part of my learning process. Nonetheless, that does not mean that I need to continue along those lines, I reflected. Times have changed, my years have passed, and my well of gathered "wisdom" has gotten fuller. What does this mean? Has endurance disappeared? No, not at all, but it has gotten a softer flavor. It almost feels like one of those beneficial yoga stretches. There is the elongated stretch where strength is felt as a natural presence, enhanced by the embraced alertness of the mind. Yes, I sigh deeply, this is what endurance means and how it should be applied in my life now. Certainly not meaning, that from now on, I will stand on my head all day or practice one of the many marvelous poses of yoga at a too extended length of time, but I now can see that the overdoing of my prior system of "endurance" with its emphasis on "doing and doing and doing" trapped my sense of natural endurance into a static place of stress. It has outgrown me, and now it seems, that with a sigh of relief, I have detected the strong, patient, caring, and wise part of endurance that is now manifesting in the silent strength of being rather than doing.

Like the tree I stand,
like its branches I extend,
like its roots I manifest strength,
like its patience I endure...
All is well - I have learned!

Son:

Wow momma, how much you have endured! It's truly remarkable also to think of how much your mother, my grandmother (whom I wish I could have met) had to endure to keep the daily lives of the whole family going. Sounds like she was the oil in the family motor that kept the comfort and activities of all flowing smoothly. And certainly, this was to the detriment of her own comfort. Such is a mother's love. How much it endures is quite staggering, if one honestly thinks about it.

I can't help but recall how much you endured as well that was most definitely underappreciated. I often tell people how you practically did everything around the house. You so lovingly and patiently made breakfast, lunch, and dinner for all of us (two kids, Dad) every single day for what seems like a countless number of days. Preparing, cooking, setting the table, and putting it all together. After we would consume your labor of love, your work wasn't over. You then would clear the table, wash the dishes, and organize the kitchen. Looking back, I feel enormous guilt that I didn't help you more. I think we might have all taken you for granted. You did all the laundry, kept the house clean, made the beds, prepared us for school, and often had some paid work as well to mix in with all your unpaid, unending household chores. I know that I could not have endured such an imbalanced relationship where one side does pretty much everything around the house. And to make matters worse, we would often yell at you from across the house if we were thirsty or hungry. And then if you brought the requested items, God forbid if it was during a crucial moment in a video game. Then, very ungratefully, I'd blame that on you as well. So unfair. I sincerely apologize for all the moments that I didn't appreciate you enough. There are countless such moments. You deserved far better. How you had the patience to deal with all of that so graciously and lovingly is a miracle upon miracles. It truly embodies the strength, love, patience, and endurance of the feminine spirit. Women have been so vastly underappreciated in many societies for far too long. The fortitude, love, and exquisite beauty of the feminine aspect, the female touch on life has come to a point of almost being smothered out and crushed by overbearing masculinity. Many of us men might not have acknowledged this undeniable, superhuman force that is womankind. Perhaps, we don't want to see that often it is she that has the unimaginable strength that we might proclaim to possess. Somehow, this needs to be balanced out in the world. Women endure giving birth, endure hormonal menstrual cycles, often endure being seen primarily externally, and in many parts of the world, endure being seen as merely a second class below men. Even in our more modern societies of this world, the female/male dynamic is promulgated in a most unhealthy fashion by so-called "reality" TV, music videos, popular music, and the media. Both masculine and feminine need healing in the world today. A woman needs to be appreciated and free to be as she is. A creature of depth, beauty, intensity, emotionally expansive, sensitive, strong, and tacitly delicate. As men, we need to soften into this paradigm, be courageous enough to humble ourselves so as to be able to understand her better. We need to realize that the so-called "macho" approach to members of the other sex isn't macho at all. It's weak. It's a way to objectify women without having the courage to dive deeper emotionally. It's actually quite cowardly behavior. It is the opposite of strength. It takes more vigor to treat people with respect, to be open, honest, vulnerable, and loving. Any other actions are a sign of fear, hiding behind a wall of false manhood, proclaiming masculinity where none exists. It takes a lot more heroism to cry when sad or in love, to fearlessly display what is in your heart than to hide behind a "manly" persona of showing only angry or competitive feelings. It's as if courage and strength have been turned completely upside down, and true courageousness is now seen as weakness. Being in touch with and open about one's internal states of being takes much more fortitude than hiding behind a wall of falsely perceived, incorrectly defined, modern masculinity. Women have long been leading in this ability to be forward, open, and vulnerable. It's time for us men to meet our counterparts halfway, lend a loving, helping hand as they lend us theirs, and both be held in a space of healing love, appreciation, and mutual admiration for the qualities that each side brings to complete the flow of unbroken life force in all its aspects. Women, like you Mother, have endured enough. It's time for us men to endure some self-reflection and to help bring back some much needed healthy balance into this sacred feminine/masculine dichotomy. May the world be healed of any toxic imbalance that has persisted in this realm. That is one of the intentions calling forth at this time. Love and respect to all, always.

Dreams

Mother:

My eyes can't believe what they are seeing... large prairies without anything on the horizon. I am spellbound as I watch the images on the small TV screen at one of our neighbor's homes in my childhood village in Holland. The space, oh my God, the space... is what took my breath away. I simply could not imagine that there were places like that on this earth. And it continued with the watching of the immense mountains of Colorado, Utah, etc., and oh, by golly, those freeways with six or more lanes, and the enormous blue waters of the Pacific Ocean. My age was about eight or so. My country, as you well know, is super tiny and everything in it does seem like a miniature world compared to what we have here. Imagine that - the first glimpses of America, for me, was the TV series of Bonanza! How cute is that! To watch those brave men zooming off into the endless prairies on their fabulous horses, made me not only dream during the day, but at night as well. Somewhere, during those fascinating hours of being exposed for the first time to the New World, was born the fervent desire to find these places, and make myself land in that Land of the endless Horizon. The dream had started and the path towards it commenced its silent unfolding. Several years later, when I had discovered the beauty of dance and was engaged in a solid training of ballet, I once again came upon a clear calling through what I had witnessed. I was still very young, maybe 12, 13, or somewhere around there. The ballet school for the advanced was giving a performance at a local theater. I sat in one of the front rows. After several numbers of classical ballet, the stage darkened once more, and out of the silence came forth from behind the stage wings... a mesmerizing sound. It was rhythmic footwork - truly haunting. I had never heard anything like that (don't forget we had no TV, and my visits to my neighbors were only about one hour per week to watch the screen). It was followed by hand clapping in perfect sync with the footwork. Then, the two ladies appeared, one close to the other; they were wearing great Spanish hats, short jackets, and beautiful skirts. I honestly believe that I never breathed throughout that incredible dance. It was my first introduction to flamenco. Needless to say, somewhere in my heart, mind, and soul, the desire to become a flamenco dancer had taken root. The dream had started and the path, little by little, and quite long (haha!), was cleared. And so it goes, on and on... and on and on..! Dream after dream seemingly born within my soul, a shy whispering into my ears about these grand experiences, not being able to believe that this could happen to me. But nonetheless, it was planted.

At the age of 25, I made my way to the expansive shores of California, against all the advice of friends and family, but there was no stopping me! Still bright is the memory in my mind, when I, for the first time, entered one of those very extended beaches of California. My soul truly soared high, and I remember that I twirled around with my arms extended wide in total ecstasy... I felt an enormous freedom. The space embraced me like a warm blanket and lifted me high to a dimension that felt like a homecoming. My dream had come true.

After having left Holland behind as well as my routines of dance, ballet, and a short teaching of flamenco, I picked up ballet again in California for a limited time, because soon I found myself engaged as a busy mother. I did dance a little bit of flamenco during those years - but too short to mention. And then, lo and behold, after all those years of motherhood, etc., my path got crossed once again with the opportunity to learn more of flamenco. And so it started – my age was 58!

*Never too late for dreams to come true! In short...
there it was: the incredible coming together with
the semi-retired flamenco dancer from Colombia,
now known as your stepfather! Quickly and
feistily, I dove into the meticulous complexity of
flamenco. Soon, I was sharing the stage with him
at many, many places, breaking his "retirement"
as a dancer with great enthusiasm!*

*The glorious moment that remains forever
imprinted on my mind, happened around the year
2016 or 2017. We were contracted to perform our
flamenco show at this most beautiful place
overlooking the Pacific Ocean. Our backdrop of
the stage was that breathtaking view of the grand
expanse of the ocean. At some point in one of my
solos, I turned my back to the audience and did a
few steps towards the back of the stage. As I
turned to do so, here I was confronted with that
amazing view. Instantly, my mind flew back to the
little girl daydreaming in Holland about living in
California, and also about becoming a flamenco
dancer. Here the two dreams merged. Glorious
was that recognition, confirmed more deeply by
the overwhelming response of the audience (two
hundred spectators), who gave us a standing
ovation with a long line of people afterwards to
thank and embrace us. My dreams had come true,
but this was way more than I could have ever
imagined..!*

So, after watching these sort of amazing happenings, I can't help but wonder what exactly takes place? As time goes on, I feel the notion rising that it might not be my fervent longing or desires that made their manifestations come to me. The possibility of there being a blueprint sent with me when descending on Mother Earth seems quite logical to me. In other words, the emerging of the steps to be taken according to the drawing, announces itself, and the views of these roads were becoming more visible to my hazy eyes. And with that, the necessity of the longing for it was created to fulfill the arduous manifestation of the blueprint. Maybe for that reason, the popular saying, "follow your heart," is actually based on that logic. The mind gets so lost in wanting and insisting on so many things, but they might be outside the blueprint. It is my heart which is connected with my specific blueprint – the call has always been much clearer and filled with joy. A manipulated decision, or conclusion, has always proven to me to lead to a dead end.

You might ask me… "and, Mom, do you still have dreams?" And I will respond, "you bet ya!" Who knows what the blueprint has drawn out in details for the remainder of my earthly days? All I know is that I still love to dream, and in my dreams I see a lovely place surrounded by beautiful nature, silence, and many high spirited, light loving people and animals, and maybe finally financial security. It is the natural, logical way of life, where dreams are allowed and embraced without fearful insistence, without hesitation, without stress – a sweet ride on life's playful waves.

Son:

Dreams

Dreams, reaching into another dimension
Is it here or there, reality extension
Waves of subconscious, passing through
Listen to conscience, you'll know what to do
Messages from the other side, or all sides one
All in the mind, or destined to be done
Are the dreams just desires, wants, and needs
Or streams must followed for a soul's deeds
Inspired or conspired, how do we know
Through life's fires, we melt the snow
Revealing the teaching hidden by flakes
Through thoughts reaching, bitten by snakes
But do not fear these phantom bites
My dear, just lots of darkness to light
There might be strain, or there may be pain
But what you gain is mastery over the slain
False idols dead upon the battlefield
No longer fed as you don your shield
Ideas of who and what you are

Fallen to new dreams from afar
Stand up proud, claim the token
Say it loud, I cannot be broken
That which can't be kept, not worth keeping
Messages while we slept, slowly seeping
Eroding away that which doesn't stay
Day by day, see fading of the fray
Rise above, riding the clouds
Live in love, discarding shrouds
Life only seems to be an exalted mystery
When we continue to repeat a faltered history
All that we could ever hope to learn
Always given to those that yearn
The truth like raindrops in a monsoon
Everywhere, like an omnipresent tune
Freeflowing from each and every direction
Ready to teach, if that be the selection
Don't worry, don't fret, no need to stress
It comes, if you let, in a lovely light dress
Awaken, awaken, stretched and shaken
Dust yourself off and say 'OK then'
I no longer wish to join the playpen
Even if it be with all the king's men
The imagination has, at times, it seems
Led us to believe we can't wake from dreams
Set an alarm one moment from now
Not necessary to doubt or ask how
No need to count any more sheep
Follow the dreams and wake from sleep

Elements/Senses

Mother:

Have you ever thought about the unique expressions and characteristics of the elements on our Mother Earth? They are all so different and so fascinating. The earth of our planet with its solidity and yet its magnificent nurturing nature. So steadily here, yet quite possible of moving! The water, our seas, oceans, rivers, creeks, and rain, delightfully refreshing and life sustaining, yet deadly when found in its wild rage. Then there is the air filling our lungs and pulsating through our bodies making us aware of the breath divine. Blowing gently to cool our warm days or forcibly creating havoc and countless debris. Fire, with its amazing quality of heating our cold homes, offering us the ability to warm the stoves and let us prepare food, or destroying everything in its path.

One day, I played with the thought about which one of these basic elements I would choose to be if that possibility would be offered... haha! I actually didn't have to think long or hard, it would undoubtedly be the wind! I immediately felt myself floating away on this sort of breathless movement of free flowing air. How incredibly wonderful that would be. I love its invisibility yet it's sweetly tangible. To go from tree to tree, from plant to plant, from flower to flower, letting the birds soar on my ethereal waves, or brushing through somebody's hair leaving my formless footprint behind, felt and appreciated consciously or subconsciously. Yes, definitely that is the one I would choose. Of course, I shudder to think of my own potentiality as wind. Unfriendly it would be to manifest as a hurricane, tornado, or desert winds... to uproot trees, houses, creating an angry sea, or relentlessly spreading the immense fires and leaving the deadly footprint of my immense power. But maybe, then again, the polar possibilities are always present in any of the elements as well as our own "element" as a human being. But as a human being I also do not focus so much on my potential of being destructive, so I am leaving that equation out of my playful choosing of being the wind.

The Wind

I wish to be the wind
that gives you the breath of life,
I wish to be the wind,
which you will receive as a breeze
easing your day
and making you remember that all things pass
and gentleness is the movement of life,
when we discover its usefulness.
I wish to be the wind,
the one that shows you
that the answers are blowing on its invisible
wings
I wish to be the wind
so I can embrace you with love,
without questions.
I wish to be the wind...
and this wish is blowing in the wind...

Son:

An excellent chapter mother. Very poetic in the essence that you brought through. I will be taking it in quite a different direction. For me, for some reason, pondering the elements of creation gives me insight into the senses that perceive those elements. So rather than call the chapter just "Elements" as you brought through, I think it would be apropos to make it "Elements/Senses" as my part will not be about elements at all.

The way that we are aware of the elements is through touch, sight, smell, sound, and taste. These are the five basic senses that govern our perception of the world. The way that I see it, it's like the five sides of a pyramid. Four walls and a base. I would say that touch would be the base, because feeling through the body, whether it be pleasure or pain is what often grounds us most into the physical plane. The other four senses add stability and help solidify the perception of being locked into the body vessel. Inside this pyramid, the sense of "I" is formed. And this "I" sense is constantly confirmed through the doorways of the five senses. I touch, therefore I am. I see, therefore I am. I smell, therefore I am. And so on. We could see the "I" as sort of encapsulated within this pyramid.

Now, let us examine each of these senses. Let's start with touch. Let us close our eyes, use earplugs if it helps to isolate the sense. Now touch anything besides our own body. Can be whatever we are sitting on, or any other nearby object. Use just one finger tip. Touch something. We feel the pressure and texture upon the skin. Does this confirm that an outside object from ourselves is there? Or is it one of the five walls locking us into that belief of separation? The sensation of touch appears upon the skin, upon the borders of the physical body. When we touch anything, the experience of that touch doesn't appear outside the pyramid. The sensation of touch always is felt inwardly, by the "I," the tactile confirmation of being. The act of touch always is perceived by the core of what we are. The five walls only make it seem like an outward event, when it's always an inward one.

Let's now take a "look" at the sense of sight. We can look out the window or look across the room. Distance appears there, space between things; some items further away, blurry even from its distance from "us." Birds fly, wind blows the leaves, all confirming an outward experience, forces outside of ourselves. This is possibly an over-used example, but it is akin to the cinema screen. The screen is there, flat and blank. When the light shines upon it, it becomes alive. It has depth, movement, color, and stories. The same is true for a painting. There are dimensions, distance, life created upon a clear, empty canvass. When we see, our eyes are like the light or paint upon the screen or canvass. The distance, space, and separation of things gives the perception of "out there." However, the cloud, the home across the way, the plants out the window, are not appearing "there." They are appearing here. No matter how far away a thing appears, its experience to us is immediate, here, now, on the lens of our eyes. The cloud doesn't appear out there in the distance, it appears instantly, presently on the screen of our perception, as does the movie on the screen. The depth and the 3-dimensionality of it all gives us this "sense" of externality. But again, it's an inward experience, helped along by the other four senses to attempt to confirm that it's an outward one. We can now combine the two senses discussed thus far. We can stand up, walk outside, head towards the things that we see. If we truly pay attention, we feel the sensation of our feet moving, the pressure on the ground. We feel arms swaying, the movement of breeze across the cheeks, hair, and skin. We get closer to the things that we see. So the two senses are confirming one another. We feel movement and we see that we get closer to that which we move towards. The reality of this experience hasn't changed from our previous experiments. It has only increased in complexity. All the sensations on the body are still perceived within. There are just more of them. That which we see, that which appears to be getting closer, also is still not seen "out there." All the colors of our vision are instantly on the surface of the eyes, here and now. These two senses alone are powerful enough to lock anyone into a perceived external experience.

Let us listen now. Is there some sound to be heard? Birds, cars, planes, kids, TV, anything? Surely, in most places, some sound is present.

Even in a quiet place, there seems to be a buzzing vibrancy of life. Sounds also often give the understanding of direction and distance. We hear something and generally know where it's coming from, approximately how far away, etc. It adds another layer of dimension and spatial awareness. You probably know where I'm going with this, but let's focus our attention onto the opening of the ears or to the space between them. Are all the sounds, no matter where they appear to originate, not processed here? Are they not heard inside the head? A distant sound is just a softer sound of a thing that would have a louder sound if we were closer to it. But both the softer and louder sound appear in the same space. All sound is perceived between the ears. The unlimited degrees of and types of sound give it depth, richness, and spaciousness. Actually, each of the senses seems to present an almost unlimited number of possible variations of experience. Maybe it is this that keeps us seeking ever new experiences. Because it is actually never-ending. The possibilities are endless.

I will now combine smell and taste here in my final dialogue on the exploration of the senses. The scents and flavors of an exquisite meal are enough to bring anyone into full corporeal awareness. Sometimes, we close our eyes, and savor the art of taste with such fervent delight, that it consumes our senses. I think, from what has been written so far, that it should be apparent that this experience, likewise, is fully internal. The rest of the senses combined lead us to believe that it is external first, then internal. But all experience is internal experience. Now, what is the point of this chapter? To convince us that the outside world doesn't exist? I can't say that. The experience of you, Mother, is also an internal one. When I hug you, I feel it in all my body, heart, and soul. My memories of us, within. My experience of us, within. The sight of you, within. My love for you, a burning fire within. The most beautiful and fulfilling experience in life is love. It opens us to new layers of perceiving. And just like the other pillars of perception, it continues internally. But it's a journey worth embarking upon. I love the experience of you, Mother. I'm grateful for all the ways in which you are perceived. Through love, I demolish the pyramidic prison of "I." Instead of seeing the senses as walls, I now see them as gateways. Gateways to perceiving love everywhere. That which might be seen as an inward experience is now an everywhere experience. No longer constrained, but free. The strings of oneness tie it all together. And love sets it all free.

Do's and Don'ts

Mother:

Venturing out into this tricky field of the above mentioned topic..! Ha... what a challenge. Not sure where the thought of this came from, but curious what the blank page has in mind for me, I now find myself sitting at the keyboard. The keyboard is truly such a sympathetic friend. It never gets to the point of simply staring at me, it seems to draw my fingers to the letters and off it goes. Such a delightful adventure! Some people call this "automatic writing." Needless to say, I do not like that word, as it sounds too robotic. To me, it is more intuitive writing. It feels like a sweet nectar that is suddenly flowing through my veins and calls me to the keyboard... in great wonder, I sit here and watch it unfold. A part of it is intoxicating because it always leaves a bit of the "nectar" behind and how delicious is that! But, I am getting off the presented subject...

Meanwhile, my stomach calls me and no matter what... it needs to be filled somewhat in order to continue the flow of words. I guess this is the first sign of the " do"... and not the don't: do eat and don't write! I'll be back soon...

My tummy is now nicely nurtured to allow me to continue the mystery of the do's and don'ts. It makes me look at the various phases of my life. As a child, my amazing mother simply did not preach the do's and don'ts. It was totally taken for granted that you knew what was acceptable and what was not. As I grew older, I found this to be a fabulous way of bringing up the children. One could simply not imagine breaking her enormous confidence in our common sense. Because that is exactly what she and my dad instilled in us. There were no rules. I was never told "be home at such and such a time"... and due to that sense of equality with her as a grown-up, I did not abuse her trust. Now, I am not going to say that I was an angel, and never did anything wrong... but that is another story. I am just talking about the topic of so-called "rules." I felt no pressure and it made me eager to act as an adult. It truly created a solid foundation for a no-nonsense base of life. Once I grew to be an adult, the sanity of this balance was definitely challenged from time to time. Out from under the protective and wise gaze of my mother, I found myself exploring some of the limits of those do's and don'ts. *How interesting to discover that the scale needed to be tipped from time to time to find out for myself where I draw lines. "You can't do this, you must do that," as a collective advice for behavior presents itself in so many areas and ways. And honestly, I was never happy with needing that to be pointed out to me. Here again, I believe, that was a natural left-over of my upbringing. Once I somehow sorted through my early grown-up years, I, as you well know, embarked with great fervor onto spiritual searches. At first, I was delighted to enter such realms of inner expansion, but soon I discovered how tricky the mind gets, and within those parameters emerged also the "set of do's and don'ts," and how these were very much pointed out by the upper-echelon of spiritual teachings. Over time, this created a disturbance within myself. I now realize that I rebel towards these defined lines of demarcation. The do's and don'ts, for me, have to be part of one flow, the wise stream that steers us into the harmonious grooves of life, without questions, with great certainty, great confidence and an ever present sense of delight. I am deeply grateful for the solid approach of my mother and father towards these stepping stones of my early life. Without realizing it at the time, and without either my mother or father being "spiritually inclined," they gave me the fertile ground of finding my own way, unhindered by the outer pressures of the do's and don'ts. A sweet example is the fact that once the topic made itself known to me to be written about, there were flutterings in the mind of what might come up or should be brought to the surface... and guess what: none of it appeared on the screen (or paper if you wish!).*

Once I had some decent food in my system, the "do write this or don't write that" disappeared and again the self-evident logic of the merged notions found its way onto the paper... and my heart is happy.

Son:

What a nice subject Mom... It's interesting to see how your Mother and your childhood family responded to that approach of no do's and don'ts. I often tell people about the secret ingredient that you used in raising us kids, your children. As many of my chapters eventually end up being about, this secret ingredient was/is love. Due to the immensity of your love, it was simply natural to not want to disappoint you. Not much discipline was needed. When one receives so much unconditional love from somebody, I think that the most obvious response is to try to be the best that we can be to stay in that loving frequency and feel deserving of it. Was I the perfect child? No, definitely not. I would, at times, get bored. And in my boredom, I would tease the dogs, finding their reactions amusing. Or, I would make ridiculous sounds or facial expressions, hoping to elicit a reaction, stretching the limits of human annoyance capacities for the sake of attention. I was just a kid with occasional bursts of energy that needed an escape route. But I would say, that in general, there was always an overarching sense of not wanting to do anything that would go against your good nature and values. You didn't necessarily give us any do's and don'ts, but through the love and the respect that you treated us with, the do's and don'ts were quite clearly felt by the properly nurtured hearts that you instilled in us. I may have pushed those boundaries of don'ts at times, as kids are wont to do. Maybe just to see how "bad" felt. And it never felt particularly good to the heart. Bad only felt good to the ego. I feel guilty about my occasional egoic approach to the dogs. It wasn't always in alignment with my deeper self. Teasing them, in some way, made me feel a sense of power over them. This has its pleasure to a lower nature. It's an ugly pleasure. A very poor substitute to the true joy found in giving and receiving love. I would say that's pretty much my only commentary at this point in my life regarding do's and don'ts. Do what is loving. Don't do what is not. That's pretty much it. And you, Mother, have been the best example in my life for this teaching. Thank you.

This subject does remind me of a program that I saw on TV once. It was a program about convicted criminals that were given the task of training dogs from a nearby shelter. These criminals were, what some might call, the "worst of the worst." They consisted of murderers, rapists, and others. Many of them were even quite terrifying to look at. Giant beasts of men with foreboding, ominous tattoos of death and destruction strewn across their bodies and even completely covering the face. Quite the intimidating image to observe. Though we strive to not judge, if one saw some of these men walking towards them on the street, one would be quite inclined to possibly changing one's direction. These were quite simply some bad looking dudes. As the TV program went on, each of these "bad dudes" was given a dog to train. I don't recall exactly how long they were given to train them, but it seems like it was somewhere between 6-12 weeks. The purpose of this program was for these men to train and better prepare these dogs for adoption and family life. They fed them, trained them to respond to commands, to behave well on a leash, not to bite or jump, etc., etc. They also kept the dogs in their cells at night to sleep with them. For many of these guys, it was the first time in their lives that they had a pet or were responsible for one. You could see as the program progressed, that these men began to soften. They smiled more frequently, their voices became more kind, and you could see that they genuinely looked upon their new furry friends with a gentleness in their eyes. Towards the end of the show, it came time for the now fully trained dogs to be returned to the shelter, being now more adoptable. It really moved me to see the reaction of these hardened men. Most of them were in tears. They were truly having a really hard time saying goodbye to their companions. You could tell that they really loved them, and the dogs, likewise, loved the men. Many of these guys exclaimed that they had never felt such unconditional love in their lives as they had from these delightful creatures. These "beasts" of men suddenly looked as innocent as a child losing a teddy bear. Their love was real. I felt an immense compassion for them. It's not hard to imagine that their lives went in difficult directions for the simple fact of having never felt unconditional love before. Who knows what kind of toxic childhood that they might have endured? It isn't difficult to surmise that if their home life was not a healthy one, that they likely went looking for a sense of family or brotherhood in some other place. Perhaps joining a gang seemed like a place to belong. A sense of community was probably sought. Often, to prove oneself "manly" enough to join these gangs, one must commit unspeakable acts. These acts usually give a sense of power to the ego. Power over another life or person. However, egoic directions tend to close off the heart. In a life devoid of love, the heart's guidance to the do's and don'ts gets shut down. These poor men were, in all likelihood, just looking for love. Approval by other men for terrible things was mistaken as a form of love. It is a very low form of ego love, devoid of any real love at all. Had these guys had some sense of unconditional love at an earlier stage in life, their stories might have been very different. Viewing this program made me hear anew the statement by Jesus of "forgive them Father, for they know not what they do." The thing that these men were most "guilty" of was ignorance. They simply sought love, acceptance, joy, and a sense of family in the wrong places. This is the case with all choices in the "don't" category. Any chosen path in the "don't" direction are attempts to fill some perceived void, just being done in an unhealthy way. In this way, forgiveness can be seen as a natural response to the misguided ways of a lost soul. If we always knew the best option to true joy, love, and peace in our hearts, I think all of us would make better decisions. But even knowing, sometimes we do just need to get burned to learn not to touch the fire. And even the decisions in the "don't" direction get us ever nearer to figuring out how to find the "do" path. The path of "do's" seems to be clearer and more easily encountered when love has been allowed to flourish in one's life. From the heart, clarity is often felt when confronted with options. The heart feels somewhat more open or expansive when the "do" path is pondered or meditated upon. Sometimes, even when we have this clarity, we don't choose the clear choice. Often, denying this clarity is due to fear. Fear of the unknown, fear of being vulnerable, fear of loss, or some other manifestation of fear that prevents us choosing the way of the heart. In conclusion, it seems to me that the choices before us in almost any circumstance are love/selflessness and fear/ego. Fear is usually the "don't," except where protection of life is concerned. And love, unconditional love, the calling from the heart is always a "do." We can "don't" or we can "do," the option is always ours to make. I hope we always choose the path of do and of love, which are often one and the same.

Tenderness

Mother:

I'm loving your amazing response to the prior topic! I am so glad to see that you felt the same way that I did about my parent's upbringing, and that I succeeded in instilling the same in you guys. It is an honor to have you as my son..! It connects really beautifully into my next topic. I am sure you will like it!

Tenderness

Every morning, I find a glass of freshly squeezed orange juice on my night stand… it feels as if silently my husband is saying, "welcome to this new day, all is well." I look over and squeeze his hand, we both smile, and I let myself be taken into his arms while he strokes my hair gently. My day has begun… and tenderness has put its mark on this early beginning of greeting the sunrise.

The "chore" of making the coffee and some breakfast has fallen away, because I wish to continue the woven thread of tenderness, and with love and care, I prepare our first meal to be taken in bed. All of this remains in silence, and no words are necessary, because the joy of being is felt. So true have been his words spoken to me many years ago. We talked about love and what a healthy relationship is all about. He said that if one engenders tenderness in the soul of the other, that this is the most important part of a relationship. If tenderness remains being inspired by the other and grows, we have found real love. If that fades out, the togetherness becomes stale, and the separation between two people has already begun. This has proven to be so true. We have cherished our sense of tenderness very much, and thereby allowed it to grow wordlessly. The words, "I love you," are basically becoming obsolete because the actions of tenderness speak louder.

I have loved to discover how it manifests in various ways. A perfect synonym for me is gentleness. It springs forth from this sense of tenderness. I remember specifically one moment where my "tenderness" was challenged. As is the case with all couples (I assume?!), that there are areas where one does not agree with the other person's opinion about the different subjects in life. And one of those came up in him with quite a *rebellious and fierce force. Not towards me, mind you, but just his anger in general about a certain injustice found in the world. It always chokes me when this sort of negativity emerges and pollutes, in my opinion, the atmosphere. I felt the sense of reaction come up in me, but somehow there was suddenly a sense of tenderness for his suffering. At that moment, I decided to remain silent, and from that silence, I could detect clearly the inner wound within him; as I felt this gentle approach towards him, I took in his words with great alertness, and I will never forget how he literally transformed before my eyes. His whole being suddenly softened, his story started to change, and soon a sweet smile embraced his face. At that time, the wound had disappeared, and it was the gentleness within me that had brought me the art of listening at that moment. But please, do not think that I have this wondrous attitude at all times! I am not a saint, but having those incredible obvious moments has been so helpful in recognizing that tenderness is the ultimate expression of love and can change everything.*

A favorite story from my man is the one of something beautiful that he had witnessed many decades before. There had been a small accident on the road, a slight running in from one car to another. The man, who was hit, came barging out of the car waving his arms in anger. The man, who was the guilty one, came out of his car, expressing with his arms that he was so sorry, and displayed a most genuine, sincere smile. So much so, that the other man changed completely and it all became a friendly event. My man has never forgotten that magic smile. He refers to it very often. Now, isn't that so amazing, that one little smile from at least fifty years ago, on another side of the world, still has this enormous impact! How far gentleness reaches and travels the globe! He saw this so long ago, he told me about it many times, and I now find myself talking about it..!

*Tenderness...
the sweet name of Love,
the Glow of Gentleness,
the invisible, indivisible stream
of the tangible mystery recognized as Love.
It provides us with
ease, warmth and space...
it is called forth from the force
of unreasonable compassion...
wordlessly, inexplicably, it lays upon
our shoulders
the sweet blanket of security,
of certainty,
of unconditional gentleness...
we are swayed by Love
and the Path of Tenderness
continues and continues...*

Son:

What a lovely chapter about this tenderness and gentleness, this softness around the edges of our being. What a great quality to pay attention to and cultivate. If we focus our attention on being more and more tender, we not only soften the rough edges of our own tendencies, but as you saw, it echoes into the world and to those around us. And this tenderness is expressed and holds the space around us in such a light and kind manner. It's the sweetest pathway to healing. I don't have a tremendous amount to add to the subject other than a poem that I wrote that embodies tenderness in a relationship...

<u>Tenderness</u>

Gentleness and tenderness
Like a lover's soft caress
Brushing across the cheeks
Lightness of touch, the lover seeks
Carry me within your giant heart
Let us be as one, never to part
Share with me all your troubles and woes
I will love you fully, through highs and lows
Your secrets are safe, this lover knows
When your spirit rises, mine also grows
Take my hand, hold my gaze
Here I stand, for all your days

Your heart against mine, feels like fire
How your eyes do shine, and inspire
A tenderness in me, a higher desire
To see you free, your soul entire
Just be, my love, rest here with me
In the silence is where we shall see
That this gentle love has the ability
To beat our hearts in combined unity
Falling away into a space of tranquility
Every way, each day, for all eternity
This stream of kindness has no end
As long as we stay open, ego suspend
Conduits of a much higher stature
An angel might be your truest nature
I call upon you to fully descend
Into this realm, to truly begin
To shine through to your highest potential
The world needs your love, so very essential
You're safe, you're loved, completely supported
Former selves, irrational fears, easily aborted
Inside this space of loving tenderness
We shall soar into a heaven of bliss
Boundless, expansive, totally endless
Brick by brick, we build a divine fortress
The love we share, sublime, impenetrable
Like a Valentine, be mine, incomparable
Rest your head from your weary travels
On my chest, let it all fully unravel
No worries, no pain, nothing more to gain
In this perfect circle of love, sweet as sugarcane

Join me in the warmth... of the sun
Lying in the fields, where it all begun
Fields of abundance, joy, light, and vibrance
We have this sense of love's might and substance
Complete, reciprocal, mirrored, cyclical
Meet the immortal, love unequivocal
Come with me into the wonderful, open
wilderness
Do not worry, the path is lain with petals of
tenderness

Escape

Mother:

Yeah, one of those days... totally overcast, gloomy, heavy, thick clouds, fog, a sense of drooly rain falling at any moment. No sign of sunshine, no rush of a breeze, trees silent and looking a bit ominous today. Maybe they are wordlessly predicting an upcoming storm. They have their own language, you know. Looking at all of this, I wonder how can I escape? And ha... gotcha... you might have thought that I was talking about the weather outside, but guess what? No, I fell into describing my state of mind... how about that!? It feels like the perfect description and it actually is fun trying to use the characteristics of nature to feel deeper into my present state of being, my dark sullen state of mind. Mind you, I do like to exaggerate! It brings forth the point that I try to make, and at the same time, it somehow lightens the imaginary load. All

of this, I guess, leads us to the topic of "escape."
On which I truly have little to say on a day like
this, other than the fact that it is what I would like
to do, to escape these feelings. What can I do to
escape these? Well, over time I have learned to
first of all, as you well know, since we have
touched upon this before, is to simply accept that
they are here - over and out. That is about it, for
trying to "escape" will get the situation actually
more tricky and laden with negativity. Having
said that, I simply wanted to share with you what
I did this morning after finding myself in this
unfriendly "climate." I remember once how a
lovely poem came through when I asked for some
sincere "help" from the Light Guides from above.
I always love to go back and reread it, as I did
this morning. So my escape turned out to be just
that... and here is the poem, they told me the
following:

Clarity and Certainty

Capture the clarity of this simple fact:
the next moment has no substance yet,
no scenario has yet entered into view,
no memories beg to be repeated,
nothing, no thing...
everything is waiting for your creation,
its openness invites you to realize
that you are not chained to habit,

its freshness calls on you to bring forth
something unheard of,
something to be worthy of celebration,
something that shines forth the
intent of this Life...
a pristine expression of All That You Are...
Welcome to Here and Now...
this is our meeting point,
we are always awaiting you...
I like this "escape"...
it holds the promise of everything and
the gentleness of its supreme potential.
The thought of it drapes me sweetly
and I can relax... I have escaped.

Son:

Well Mother, it seems that we are definitely at times in sync. I was also in quite a state of soul funk (not the musical kind) yesterday morning when you sent me this chapter. A lot of things were worrying me, causing anxiety and fear. And, as is often the case, by the end of the day, there was a complete reversal, and then I was on top of the world! So... how did I escape? My method of escape in this particular case was simply by being as honest with myself and my partner as humanly possible. Openly displaying and laying bare what was troubling my soul. Having somebody to feel comfortable enough to share all of yourself with can be a truly healing experience. Mother, you already know that I'm dating Ms. Lovely, as I'll call her here. But for others that might read this, the truly compatible soul that I spoke about in the "pain" chapter has come back around and we officially started dating about one month ago. It has been, as expected, very deep and intense. We have had numerous amazing journeys, talks, experiences, and soul stirring rapid growth fires to pass through in quite a short time. We have found enormous healing through complete transparency and honesty. Every time that we are vulnerable enough to share our emotions, thoughts, and feelings with each other, we grow ever closer, with deeper levels of connection, trust, and love. Yesterday, we both realized that we are kind of exhausted. But like a soul level exhaustion. We were both in a quite unpleasant state yesterday morning. Through tenderness, love, and honesty with each other, we found our escape route for that particular situation. We both discovered that we have been dealing with heavy doses of fear. For me, it has been fear of losing her, fear of not being worthy of such a vibrant, beautiful being, fear of running out of things to talk about... so many things. Through bringing those fears out into the open, I was able to track down exactly the source of my tiredness. I started to feel my heart wanting to open more towards her, being met with a constant tension in my chest, fighting that expansion, trying to keep my heart protected and safe. Loving very deeply can be truly scary and vulnerable. I see so much potential with Ms. Lovely that I find myself with a level of fear that I have never known. I've had fears in relations before, but this is another level. And this constant battle between my heart opening, and fears trying to keep it closed, has been wiping me out. It's a constant level of anxiety that I didn't perceive until yesterday, through talking about it, acknowledging it, and observing it. I found a lot of the fears lifting during this process. For her, it was very much a lot of the same emotions accompanied with guilt for being so afraid. And when I opened up about my fears, it made her feel less guilty for her own feelings and created a space of healing for us both. I could, at that point, quite viscerally feel my heart opening, and the pattern of fear trying to close it back down again. But now that it was seen so clearly, I could consciously choose to not let it shut me down. I was sitting taller, opening my chest, breathing awareness and light into my heart space, and permitting the sense of an expanded heart to have its way without fighting it. I finally started to feel more free. A level of relaxation came over me and between us that neither of us had felt before. My heart has been burning ever since, and an increased sweetness and love between us has been the oh so rewarding result. It feels deeper, more open, and my soul no longer feels the exhaustion of continuous inner battling. So, our escape from the internal funk of fear-dom was to let the funk out, expose it, share it, and deal with it compassionately between each other. With this method, a new, lighter, and more loving internal reality emerged. Hallelujah!

Now, when I was single, I had other "escape" methods. Those methods varied at times. My ultimate escape route was always the idea of running into the woods, living off of nuts and berries, and finding a cave detached from the world! Haha! But luckily, I never reached that extreme of need for escape. My true methods for dealing with those "dark" days were not so different than my method with Ms. Lovely. It usually consisted of being honest with myself, examining my internal state, and trying to find the source of the pain within. Then, through questioning, love, or meditation, trying to find a way to bring light into that darkness. At times, there was nothing to do but to simply feel the pain, and allow myself to tremble with sorrow and cry it out. Often, it's made worse by trying to be tough about it and holding it in. Then we have a tendency to become unpleasant to those around us and externalize our pain by blaming others. It just becomes more gun powder added to the pile building up in our restricted, closed barrel within, awaiting explosion. Better to unload it before it's too late. Allowing such emotions to be felt and processed in their moments is ofttimes the quickest way to the other side.

Another, deeper, more "spiritual" approach that has also worked for me is just a deep knowing that everything is ok. Nothing can permanently harm the base of who we are. It is untouchable, always safe, loving, and completely unruffled by the changing winds of life. When I can (which is not always), tapping into this space of eternal present awareness is, by far, the most remedial escape route for any and all manifestations of unpleasantness. It brings instant clarity, no self-doubt or repudiation, and really no egoic self to be troubled whatsoever. Some lingering of skunk funk might appear, it just no longer touches the ground. It just kind of blows around in the spaciousness of being until it dissipates. Of course, I cannot always do this. Sometimes, the walls of suffering are too thick to be able to see the other side. That's when just sitting with it, and allowing it to be felt and processed might be the only remaining route option. But there's always an escape. Freedom and love are our true natures. Nothing too funky can last forever. Knowing this to be true already makes finding the escape hatch a good bit easier, not adding such a weight of seriousness and reality upon the "darkness" as might possibly be felt otherwise. Freedom is the ultimate escape and it's always here, and always available. And actually, paradoxically, we can't escape our freedom! Ha!

Poetry

Son:

What is poetry? What is poetic? How does the poet find it? Is it limited to the breathtaking and majestic facets of life? Or can it be encountered through a renewed poetic vision of sorts? I can remember one day in India about 22 years ago that I had, perhaps, one of my most poetic moments. And it was quite atypical to what one might typically consider poetic. I had listened to a two hour long cassette tape (yes, I'm that old) of the first discourse that I'd ever heard from Eckhart Tolle. It truly transported me to a space of pure awareness and near thoughtlessness. I distinctly recall one moment that occurred soon after having listened to that. I was walking down one of the dusty, made of dirt side streets, wide enough for maybe two rickshaws. There was an unsightly six-foot tall cement wall to my right. It was mostly gray, with hints of ages old, faded into the grayness paint, peeling away. Random and mostly torn parchments of various advertisements were also waving gently at their torn edges as time slowly stripped them from their foundation and of their color. Even bits of cement were broken off in various parts, with their own stories to tell. Along the base of the wall were random piles of garbage, bags ripped apart by a hungry variation of street creatures, having spread the contents in haphazard fashion across all segments of the roadway. Everything was also covered in light brown, adobe-colored desert dust. The hot sun was piercing through several layers of skin, reaching an uncomfortable depth as it drew out perspiration from the body, its desperate countermeasure to the penetrating heat. Perhaps the bodily fluid was just boiling to the outside of the inside. A few blocks down, I could see a lanky ox. Bony, long legs, skin hugging the ribs, and a dented, oversized and misshapen bell dangling from its weary neck. To my left were dust laden, dull colored, two and three level residential cement buildings in varying states of disrepair. There were also healthy and unhealthy looking piles of excrement from all sorts of life scattered throughout the vicinity. The aroma in the air confirmed this fact. That scent combined with the smell of mixed garbage was one aspect of the experience through the nose.

There was also the dry dustiness that left the internal of the nostrils feeling as if the air was attempting to lay down a new desert land within my lungs and nose as well. And lo and behold, I stopped there in this spot, as my eyes filled with tears... My mind was so devoid of thought or judgment about this experience, that I perceived the utter uniqueness of the moment. I don't think that there was anything in that experience that would conventionally be considered beautiful. But it was. It was poetic in its beauty. There was a silence beneath it all. Time stood still. It was seen as a painting, art, arising from the creative silence. That exact moment, with all of its sights, smells, and sensations were only experienced precisely in that way only through the filter of my perception, never to be repeated again! What wonder! Even this externally, normally defined dull landscape, was fully alive with uniqueness, vibrating with life and sensations, miraculous in its appearance! I was fully present in that moment, as I saw and perceived fully through each of my senses. The experience was rich in its depth from every angle of perception. Without the labels of ugly or pretty, hot or cold, stinky or floral, it was simply experienced as a conglomeration of unique stimuli, as an expression of unlimited divine potential. In that instant, I was a witness to this one of a kind artwork from the brush that paints all of life. And to me, it was exceptionally beautiful. Its shocking beauty was enough to startle me, grab my steps, and overwhelm me with emotions of love and gratitude as I took in the grandeur that was seen in that unsuspecting place. Poetry can be like that. It can flow from the most unsuspected places about unsuspecting things. It can be expressed in any way whatsoever. Its expression attempts to convey the originating flavor, to transfer some semblance of the poetic essence. The essence wafts into the senses of those that follow, creating a new stream of poetry through each unique and aware point of being, in an endless cycle of poetic experience. Poetry is life and life is poetry.

I stop

I walk, I stop
I think, I stop
Who's here, I'm not
Who walks, I forgot
These thoughts for naught
Just sounds that were taught
I sought a lot
I jot in this spot
Words are being outshot
Coming like an onslaught
I wring what I wrought
I sing what was brought
Getting hot and distraught

Trying to untie the knot
Of life's mysterious plot
But it's tied so taut
What time have you got?
Oh, it's NOW, on the dot?
The moment's been caught
How poetic, I stop

Mother:

Loving the subject... of course! As I sit here and watch whatever it is that comes forth on this topic, I feel foremost the sweetest silence. It is just that, a humming, actually hardly a humming, a whisper maybe of a humming, still described as silence but yet it is not. It almost feels like there is a deep agreement between the soul and the mind. There is silent interaction, wordlessly agreeing on the sparkling essence that they share. An essence of sacredness. They both, the soul and the mind, nodding their heads and smilingly imbibing in this nectar of pristine aliveness. Through this interaction, the heart awakens and wants to join in, it opens itself up, and allows the joy to be expressed through her unique way, and poetry is born. This is what comes up for me. It is the intense joy which I experience again and again when called to write poetry. I remember vividly many years ago, I should say decades ago, I was very clearly called to write. It was somewhat of a daunting task at that moment. I had said that if I was supposed to write, that the opportunity would have to present itself clearly. At the time, we had the whole family living at home and there did not seem to be any opening for me to work quietly on this calling. Within about two weeks' time, everybody got an evening job! Suddenly, the road cleared immediately and I had, of course, to follow my "directions." And yes... I obeyed, bought a notebook, and sat myself down that first evening with pen in hand, and a stomach with a bit of nervousness. I had no idea what it was going to be or how it would come about. Never will I forget the whiteness of that blank sheet of paper... but it turned less and less stark and somehow that whiteness and the supreme silence seemed to open up my heart, mind and soul. And a sweet, swaying humming announced itself, and before I knew it, I was writing away and the sense of peace, joy, and exhilaration elevated me higher and higher. The closing of the chapters were made very clear by a certain hand motion, almost like a form of signature. And always, I was deeply grateful for this outpouring. The first thoughts that came to me after I was done were always that my fervent wish was that whomsoever would read those words, might feel the same heightened sense of awareness, of the nectar that had been allowed to drip through my being and into the pen, that it would be given to partake for the readers as well. Remembering that wondrous intention makes me think of something I read some years ago. The fabulous, incomparable poet, writer, philosopher of Uruguay, the late Eduardo Galeano, told his story about a research he once did in the libraries of France. I believe it was Paris. I'm not totally sure about the exact details, neither what the search was for... haha. All I remember is what he found. He had spent many, many days and countless hours going through the books at the library, and just when he was about to give up, he came upon this one sentence which opened up everything for him. The sentence explained to him that "paper is God's skin," it carries its words not only across the globe, but also continues for centuries to come! How sacred is this statement, this sentence! How incredibly beautiful is the expression that finds paper, wafts its melodic waves on the winds, and reaches the inner temples of our eager minds, softens our hearts and allows our souls to find themselves. It is like you say, the ordinary becomes extraordinary. I would say that poetry allows for a harmonious alignment to the essence of my being. The mind, heart, and soul unite in perfect balance and the world becomes new.

Poetry

No words can describe its secret,
yet it pleads to be spoken.
This sweet contradiction,
always opening up the invisible portal,
so we can pass it in breathless awe
to encounter the Breath of Life...

The Folly of Age

Mother:

The folly of it is correct. It is that ethereal thread running through the hours, days, weeks, and years that somehow has itself planted in our brain, our mind, and claimed an identity. Somewhat of a silent threat, whispering that the finish line is getting closer. And if we doubt that, well, just have a look in the mirror! The solid proof of it is manifested in this body. And so, some of us shrink at the mention of age. Totally baffling, it awaits every one of us on this journey called life. I find it a most interesting part of this earthly existence. I have found that there are definitely certain facets of life for which we are not, and obviously cannot, truly be prepared for, no matter how many discourses are being spoken about them, or endless analysis written about it.

For me, one of those huge surprises was motherhood..! Wow, that just about took me for a complete loop. Read about it, heard about it, watched it close-up with other female friends that were ahead of me in reaching motherhood... and yet, oh my God, nothing and absolutely nothing had touched upon what this entailed. It has to be the rawness of the experience that we have to undergo in order for it to become a settled part within ourselves. I find that age belongs to this group as well. Here again, we hear so much about it, seemingly preparing us for that uncertain phase of life greeting us at every corner of time. By now, at the age of 70, I can say that I have had some interesting insights into this delightful, mysterious chapter of age.

Age has its various effects on us throughout the years. When we were in our first decade, oh boy, we so much wanted to be in the next decade, be teenagers and young adults. We would feel proud when people thought we were older than the number of our years indicated. Even in our twenties, this might still be the case until the frightening 30 came along. Then suddenly, there was no more mentioning of our age and we always wanted to look younger. Yes... this is when the game of hide-and-seek started to come into play. For several more decades, trying to dive under that reality was an accepted norm. To me, the most interesting curiosity came when we would enter the retirement communities to dance our shows and, lo and behold, every time, the

140

residents would be eager to tell us their age. This phenomenon, I discovered, starts normally around the age of 80. With great intensity, they would ask me: "do you know how old I am?" And always, the anxiously expected response was uttered by me... "oh my goodness, you gotta be kidding!" It seems like we are jugglers with the ball of time, sometimes we throw it up, and sometimes we proudly catch it. And so it goes, it truly feels to me as a huge contradiction, the various games of "time" or "age." It, at the same "time," stands still and moves. When I look back, I can still clearly feel how I observed the things around me, and with that same eye, I today also look and observe, and that part, without a doubt, is the same and has not "moved." Yet, the events that passed by can certainly be seen as a development of sorts.

To my great surprise and astonishment, I have to tell you, that for me, the greatest secret that life had hidden from me has been: age! The sweetness and the ease of living that I have discovered in this last decade is priceless. And that, as you well know, does not mean that I live financially well and taken care of, or that I can see life in this phase as a big glorious vacation. No - it is not that. The inner turmoil of what to do, and where to go to do it, is softly going into the background. And with that retreat into the background, there has been a gentle opening up

141

of an inner richness. For sure, I have to iterate that luckily my health is good. I do know that once I am in pain, my life falls to pieces, since I am not one who suffers well! So far, I have been very fortunate, and have enjoyed the seeming health that has been experienced for several decades.

I believe that the mystery of the more obvious uncertainties in life, when age gets higher, is actually what appeals to me. The unknown seems as a great invitation to become silently more open, to dwell in a calm alertness, and embrace a sense of unquestionable acceptance. Always, there has been uncertainty, but now it has a more immediate, inescapable flavor added to it. It brings to the foreground a great opportunity to delve much deeper into the parts of ourselves that have maybe thus far been untouched upon. I treasure these years, and find myself thoroughly enjoying the mature freshness of my aged youth.

Son:

Hmmm... interesting subject. The title of the chapter, "The Folly of Age," is very specific and difficult for me to resonate with and write about. So, I'll break it down in my mind to one word and see if it's easier to find some subject matter based on just the one word. I'll just use the word "age" and see what comes up for me...

Ok, after a few days of just sitting with this word in the background, I finally have a direction of where to go. For me, age isn't something that I've ever thought much about. It's just there, like an identifier, or mark on the wall, as if checking one's height whilst the body grows. As you also alluded to, in some ways, I don't really feel that different now as compared to 20 years ago. Something has definitely remained steady, persistent, always here. I feel as if I could still easily inhabit my 20 year old self. But aging ekes along so slowly, that if I truly dive into my 20 year old self and compare it alongside my 40 year old self, the differences and life experiences are actually oceans apart. So, as you said, there are parts of me that feel ageless and unchanged, but there's another part that has grown in leaps and bounds. I suppose that this is the normal human experience.

The only way in which age has entered into my mental sphere of consciousness is in how it relates to others in romantic relationships and also in a background pressure as time goes by to do more or achieve more. In romantic relationships, I have often dated people more than 10 years apart in age from my own. And this has been on both sides of the spectrum: older and younger. It was never an issue for me personally, as I simply considered each as a soul to which I was drawn towards regardless of the number of years assigned to the form. The only concern, albeit slight, was the potential judgment from others about it. But that preoccupation was never worrying enough to change anything. It would just manifest at times in a slight hesitation when people would inquire about our ages. But for me, love has always just been love, and if it's present, then that is the most important factor in maintaining that connection.

I would say that the biggest factor that the topic of age has had on my life is as a mounting pressure to do or accomplish more. The older that I get, the more that I feel that I should have been more successful by now. Feeling always still a little lost, looking for my place in the world, and feeling somewhat of a failure for not having really found my path yet as of 41 years of age. And that measurement of success or finding that pathway consists in some ways of more financial security. But I would say that more of that success consists in a lifelong desire of wanting to somehow make the world a better place. Not that I want to be arrogant enough to believe that I have something to offer in order to achieve that end. It's just simply, as the years go by and my heart ever expands, that there's a natural love present for all beings. And that love desires, of its own accord, to spread, to feel other people feeling it, to see less suffering and more peace everywhere. Just a simple, natural call from the core of whatever level of love exists within me to be shared. So, with each passing year, I feel more and more failing in that aspect. I feel like there's nothing more worth doing that to spread it, manifest it somehow. But I've always felt somewhat paralyzed in the space of not knowing... not knowing how to show my love. I can only hope that maybe our call to write will lead to that knowing. Maybe it is the medium through which the love wishes to be expressed. I can only pray that I honor its resonance properly onto the paper, pray that somehow, somewhere, that it might move somebodies heart to light ever brighter. If it can move many somebodies, that would be even more grand. It wishes to burn ever brighter in me, and naturally wishes to ignite a conflagration in as many hearts as possible. It's not me. It's just a natural flow, as you know, that love wishes to go and grow. That would be the greatest measure of success as this cloak of flesh gets ever more marked with the signs of age. As we both age, as the years tick on by, my deepest yearning is that we both can surrender ever deeper to the flow of pure love for all, and express it in the most unhindered way possible. If we can do that, the invisible marks on the wall that measure the growth of our souls will be a pleasure to reflect upon. The years can be fondly recollected with gratitude for every step of the journey of aging that leads us to the ever deepening peace and joy of a heart centered attempt at existence. This would be well aged indeed!

Confidence

Mother:

Terrified I was, when suddenly I found myself sharing a stage with my man, who, as you know, has been a professional flamenco dancer his entire life! And here I was, after a 30 year hiatus from dancing, clinging to anything that I could to feel worthy of being by his side. Groping at the faded out memory of the intricate technique of flamenco, its dazzling rhythms, and complicated footwork, meanwhile trying to maintain a gracious and effortless expression. Yes... quite a daunting task! I was born with a few great attributes: perseverance, determination, and self-discipline. With those weapons, I threw myself into this new challenge. But no matter how hard I tried, I somehow felt myself falling short to what I wished to feel and express. That is when I discovered the huge difference between determination and confidence. I could somehow, in a fake way, rely on my sheer will to perform the required techniques to express myself in this field of dance. The fact that I had lost 30 years of practice and experience didn't help my mind much. I took this as a given that I would remain inferior next to my man. Finally, one day, I had a serious talk with myself, and a deep look at my situation. I came to understand that I had to accept simple facts, and that was that the lost years could not be replaced by endless practice, so I had to find another doorway. I started to realize that, more than anything, I wanted to feel and be myself, without the nagging fear of not being enough. I began to analyze my form of dancing, and soon I became aware of the fact that it was the moments of stillness where I sensed a deeper part of myself. Now I began to dive deeper into that and used those moments to connect with myself. In this way, I started an interesting focus on my physical body. My heart became my concentration. I could feel that if I would focus on the heart area and give it space, that I would relax and feel connected with who I am. I would mentally draw an upside down triangle from my shoulders downwards, with the point to my heart, and feel it as if that area was a closed window, and then I would open it up! I also mentally drew an upward triangle from the bottom of my stomach, with the upper point at my heart, and again feel it as a closed window at first and then open it up, the two triangle points meeting at the heart. I would take a deep breath, settle into this seat of my heart "being," relax my body, and ask it to dance. I especially used the moments of stillness or silence to reconnect with this path of alignment. This is what became a miracle for me. I would instantly feel connected with myself, and left the mind, with its inadequate conclusions, behind... and in this way, I stumbled upon: confidence! The more that I engaged in this, the deeper and more stable that it became. I then started to use it as well in my daily life. The sweet sense of this invisible embrace of myself has become a great love in my life. When I walk on the streets, when I talk to others, this opportunity is always there, and it totally silences the distracting thoughts of worthiness or unworthiness. It somehow thrives on its own momentum of flowing freely, and thereby offering not only for oneself, but for those around us as well, this nurturing and self-evident emittance of well-being. I have come to understand that confidence indeed is our natural state, which spreads its fragrance without having a label. It gets absorbed and feeds those around us, like an unheard song, it dances through the ether and celebrates the simple sense of being, no more no less.

Son:

Another interesting subject Mother. I like it! I'm confident that others will as well. I like how you imagine the windows opening to the heart. That's a lovely way to visualize opening up to the space within.

For me, confidence is, and has been, a mixed bag in its myriad ways of showing up in my sphere of experience. There are avenues in which confidence has been fairly solid for me. Then there are other ways in which it has been seriously lacking. I've had a few experiences in my life that have had immense effects on different levels and layers of my confidence.

The first experience was back in Virginia, when I was 23 or 24 years old. At the time, I wanted very little to do with the world. I had been traveling to India repeatedly at that point since the age of 17. About three years total was spent there. I had no interest in a career, no major life goals, had never been in a relationship yet at that point, and didn't really see the point in a "normal" life. I had even considered finding a monastery and spending my life in that setting rather that deal with the troubles of modern existence. I wanted peace more than anything else. Everything else seemed empty and pointless in a way. Anyhow, there I was at the age of 23/24 after having recently returned from India. I don't remember if it was your book, or where the book came from that I decided to read that day, but I spent the entire day reading a book about "waking up." Something in that book was destroying me. An ocean of peace and an energetic firestorm were drowning me in tranquility and consuming my ideas in a raging inferno within. Many concepts that I had about my path, myself, and enlightenment were being obliterated. The words on those pages were like portals into a space of peaceful unknowing. By the time that I finished the book, "I" was gone. There was no "me" left. There was nobody there to have a concept of me, or I, or mine. I went to lie down on my bed, and there I was, but I wasn't. No thoughts crossed my mind. I was aware, without commentary. I was simply the space of being, of alive, pure aware witnessing. I was aware of the body, I was aware of a smile on the face, and I was aware of a peace that surpassed all mental understanding. I became very sensitive to a vibratory electric presence in all things within about a 20-foot radius from my physical form. I could feel that that which was alive in me was alive in all things. I felt myself as the grass outside the walls. I felt the dew upon my grass blades. I felt myself buzzing through the wood of the nightstand. I could feel the static electricity of my reality coursing through the fibers of the carpet. Everything around me was not separate from me. It was of the same thread. The field of being was not constrained by the borders that the mind creates because the mind was free; it was gone. Those borders had been smashed. Many hours, possibly the full night, passed in this way. My eyes remained opened. I did not sleep. There was no need for sleep as no energy was expended. I was energy. There was only peace and love, and an awe at the miracle of existence. When I did get up in the morning, I felt as though I'd had the greatest rest of my life. I was fully alive, my soul having been refreshed in this awakened experience, free from the burden and heaviness of a "me." The mind, as it is wont to do, did start churning its engine again that next day. But there was definitely a lighter sense of "I" that re-emerged. This lighter "I," however, did have the strange sense of being a little bit lost. My whole life, the main thing that I sought was peace and escape from the world. I had always been seeking something. On this day, I didn't know what else to seek. All I could feel was peace. But my former identity of a "seeker" felt like it had died in a large part on that glorious night. I did not know what to do next, as my former ideas and plans were now seen as futile. In this new space of clarity, I had realized that some of my motivations in longing for a monastic lifestyle were based in fear. I was afraid of facing the world and its challenges. I was afraid of people, of being hurt by people. I was afraid of relationships, not feeling worthy, and fear of loving someone that might stop loving me. I simply had been filled with a lot of fear about facing myself, my lower self, through the reflection of other humans and life in general. But this intense experience began to build or add on to a foundation of knowing and trusting that all is well, and that peace is always here and available now as our true nature. I had a new level of believing that nothing can truly effect or change this foundation except for my own mind getting lost in worries, thoughts, and emotions. So, the foundation of all that is became my solid ground, my starting and ending point for a base of confidence. However, I did possess an extreme contrast at this point in the sense of a great confidence in the nature of existence, but an ego that was still quite shy and often afflicted with a desire to please and be liked, accepted, and loved. I still had, in my mental patterns, the idea that I didn't fit in anywhere, that I was strange, and hadn't done normal things for someone of my age. All of these ideas often made me feel uncomfortable around people. I had always been a bit of a hermit for this reason. After my experience that night, and subsequent conclusion that fear was a factor in my desire to renounce the world, I had decided that it was time to just throw myself into life, just live, and overcome my fears. In a way, I wanted to test out my new levels of confidence by casting myself into the fire of experiential living. So, over the next couple of years, I saved money and prepared myself for a move to NYC! I couldn't think of a better place to hurl headlong into, in order to experience life, than the multicultural, dynamic, and never-sleeping Big Apple! And it did not disappoint! I credit NYC for, what I would say, changed me from a spiritual child into a spiritual man. You have to be pretty tough to survive 7 years in that city. It's a whirlwind of energies, people, experiences, noise, and challenges. Even though I was very shy and boyish on a personality level, on a deeper level, I still knew that a part of me was indestructible. This gave me the courage to face my surface-level fears. My first years in NYC were quite challenging indeed. Some of those challenges I discussed in an earlier chapter. There were also challenges on an ego level. I tried to make friends, tried to see what "normal" life was like. I ended up hanging out with guys that I would say were quite different from myself. I was, in some manner, trying to figure out who I was on a worldly level. So I was partying, drinking, going to clubs, dancing, and trying to pick up women with only physical pursuits in mind, as that is what the other guys were doing. After some months of this, I started to get somewhat depressed. It all felt as empty as I had imagined that it would be. It was exactly this type of empty existence that I had wanted to avoid by living in a monastery. It was missing all the things that make existing actually a pleasure. It was missing richness and depth, true human connection, and love. One fateful night, I ended up dancing with a truly lovely lady. I'm not sure how we were able to converse over the pounding beats of the music, but somehow we ended up in a spiritual or philosophical discussion. She ended up talking about how wonderful her church was and invited me to go that Sunday. Now, bear in mind that I had, at that point, read quite a bit about Jesus, including the bible, but I had never actually been to a church service before. I had always been open to truth from wherever it might be expressed. I always felt a deep connection to a guidance within, and felt that it would always lead me to where I needed to be to learn what I needed to learn. I would even have conversations as a child with this life force or compass guide within, and would feel the truth somehow respond within me. So, in a way, I was against the idea of someone telling me how I should or shouldn't be or what I should believe. In that way, church was never something that appealed to me, as I believed that a personal relationship with the divine was preferential and possible for all beings through quietness of mind and humility of heart. I thought the noise of someone explaining the bible text to me in their interpretation of what it means *to them was more likely to be a hindrance than a help. However, I had gotten a little lost in my ways at that time, and a place of worship just did sound like what the soul needed. So, I did go that Sunday. I actually have no recollection of what the preacher spoke of on that day. But it did take just a few old words to shake my soul to its core. At some point, in the beginning of the service, they said the Lord's prayer. And when they uttered the words, "Thy will be done, on Earth as it is in Heaven," I started to tremble. It hit me like a thunderbolt straight to the heart. It shocked me into a renewed state of silence. I cried uncontrollably, as I felt an immense love wash over me as I was so simply and gently reminded of how to get back on my path. The weight of the world that I had been trying to fit into was lifted off my shoulders. I knew exactly in that moment what the message was in that prayer that hit me so hard. By attempting to fit in and belong in societal circles that were not in alignment with my being, I was not being true to divine will. I was going against the flow of what wished to be expressed. I was acting in ways that were not natural for me, just to "belong" somewhere. I was not honoring my inner guidance. I felt like for God's will to be done, I had to follow my heart, stand strong in who I am, to fearlessly and humbly listen for, and tread upon, the directions that called to me in each moment of my life. This is, and always has been, a will beyond my personal will, beyond ego fears, and beyond the pressures of trying to fit in. And I most certainly had not been doing that. I left church that day deciding to not be anybody that others wanted me to be ever again. On my walk home, I felt like I was not touching the ground. I felt so free, and full of light and love. I was so happy to find myself again, as that is how it truly did feel. I had been lost, but now I was found. My mind was quiet once more. I felt peace. I immediately ended the friendships that were not in service to my heart's call. I had now reached a new height of confidence that I had not known before. I knew who I was more than ever. It is interesting, because before that day, the reactions that I got to my life stories were markedly different than the reactions after that day. Before, when I would talk about my spiritual pursuits, lack of relationships, etc., I was often embarrassed about my abnormality and this was often reflected back to me by the reactions of those listening. I used to hesitatingly try to make conversation about the few things in life that I knew something about, namely spiritual things. And the reaction was quite often a strange look on their face, or just straight up telling me that I was weird. But after that soul shocking day at church, I was no longer embarrassed about being different. I loved myself so much. I loved the liveliness that being true to my heart made me feel and I had no desire to be any different. At that point, I really couldn't be bothered by the thoughts and opinions of others. To be clear, those preoccupations did not perish completely. I still wanted people to like me to some degree, of course. Just not enough, anymore, to change and to be other than myself. At that point, when I spoke about my life, there was now a confidence behind my words, a surety of being, and a comfort in my own skin. As could be expected, now people responded to me in a totally different way. Now, they seemed more interested or wanted to hear more. Some found my story inspiring or fascinating. I was still seen as "different," but no longer in a negative way. Just different, maybe unusual, but accepted. This was the gift from that day in church. I now accepted and loved myself exactly how I was. I just simply needed that push from those words in the prayer to gain the confidence that I needed to honor myself more truthfully. And I'm so grateful for that experience.*

Going back to my deep experience in Virginia, I had gained a confidence in the foundation of all things. The moment in church shook me to a new degree of confidence, but more at a personal "I" level, an acceptance of how the foundation wished to be expressed in this story as a personality. Hand in hand, they both combined to lead me to a place of honoring my truth more freely and easily through all phases of being.

I do want to be clear that I don't want it to sound like I've reached a place where I'm confident all the time, always at peace, following a higher will perfectly, never make mistakes, or have no fears, etc. Those experiences were the two groundbreaking moments that shaped the bulk of whatever confidence that I do have. However, there are new layers of fear and blockages to being my best self that are constantly being discovered, rising to the surface to be seen and dealt with. I try not to feel guilt about my imperfections. I just try to approach them with compassion, dive into them, love them, and express them honestly rather than try to hide them or ignore them. Somehow in this process, their claws loosen, their dark shadows lighten, and day by day, we all inevitably get closer to becoming more aligned with who we wish to be and more in flow to what a deeper force of life wishes for us as well.

The last thing that I would like to mention is that, ironically, at the time that I'm writing this, that I've actually attended church for the last 4 weeks. It's not something that I ever thought that I would enjoy. But I have loved it. I have found a good number of people there that are just quite loving, and earnestly just seeking to be the best that they can be. And that is wonderful. What started this surprising 180 degree turn to my previous aversion to the idea of attending church? Well, about 10 weeks ago, I started having a longing in my heart to acknowledge the beautiful soul that Jesus Christ was/is. It kind of arose within me out of nowhere and I just decided to follow that inner guidance. I started praying at that time also, and since then, so many beautiful things have transpired in my life. I've never been one to really pray. Maybe I had some arrogance to believe that I could deal with everything on my own. However, I have found that praying has enormously softened many otherwise bumpy challenges. When I feel fear, confusion, or any other unpleasant feeling that might make me feel un-centered, I simply and humbly ask for help. I will say, "Jesus, have mercy on this fear" or whatever the situation is, and it instantly becomes easier, lighter. I find a sweetness in this asking for help from a being that I truly love and admire. Sometimes, we just simply don't know how to solve everything, or don't have the strength. But we are truly not alone, and this adds another layer of confidence that we may not possess internally. But we can have that confidence, that faith that an extra boost that we might need can come from forces outside of our little internal realities. Whether we pray to Him, or angels, or guides, or the Universe, the feeling of reaching out for a loving, helping hand just feels more honest and caring, allowing beings that truly do wish to assist us the chance to do so and show their guidance and help, and bring us even closer to a place that we can also be a better version of ourselves, which in turn just makes the world a better place for all. So, confidence, for me, has over these last 20 years, gone from foundational to personal confidence, and finally now joined with an impersonal faith. It's now a shared confidence. A confidence that if I can't do it, or can't heal something within me, or can't face some fear, that I now don't have to overcome it alone. This certainly is the sweetest and most fulfilling layer of confidence that I've discovered yet. I ask for love, ask for compassion, and I feel the response, the increased lightness of being, and it's beautiful. I thank the beings that have assisted me on my journey that led me to the experiences that gave me confidence to be true to myself, and that are aiding me to a new level of confidence that all things are possible.

Life

Mother:

With a deep sense of melancholy, I feel that the conclusion of this conversation has announced itself. It has been a journey of the heart, that is what I feel. I am endlessly grateful for you having taken on this invitation. It has lifted my soul to a great extent, and made our resonance ever more profound. What a sweet play of our words, meeting each other's expressions, dancing with the unspoken ideas, and having it spilled over onto the "skin of God," like Eduardo Galeano described as the correct description for paper! If ever anyone will read these words, I, as always, wish with all my heart and soul, that some of our contentment and happiness with which we have woven through these expressions, will find a nestling place within their hearts.

I am going to conclude my last topic with a poem that was written about seven years ago in which I describe what life has taught me thus far,

and it still holds true for me now, and probably
more deeply so at the present moment.

Life

Like the child who, through touch,
finds out that fire is hot,
ice is cold
and water is wet...
life is deductive reasoning in action.
Youth consists of the premature years of this
process of elimination.
Subconsciously, it takes us on a seeming
whirlwind ride of ever new topics,
a hurried pursuit of the "idee-fixe"
of the moment,
unashamedly hypnotized by the elusive future.
All the while, the purpose of the process is
fulfilling itself,
unbeknownst to our absorbed mind...
and over time, life cleanses us of excess,
exaggeration, and things exotic.
The whirling of the clock is slowing down...
our bowl of expectations is being emptied,
and the gentle truth is being revealed.
We discover what it is that we do not care for,
we have come to know what does not work for us,
and so the process of elimination
has come to a quiet fruition
in the springtime of the last phase of our life.

Simplicity has absorbed chaos,
contentment has made the intensity
of desire obsolete,
openness has melted the pursuit of righteousness,
today has swallowed tomorrow.
The peace of not-wanting deepens,
the joy of not-needing enlightens.
The beauty of age has silenced the tools for
sculpturing our lives,
and in this breathless silence,
the song of an unimaginable freedom
is being heard.
And while the outer beauty folds its magic wings,
the inner beauty has taken its virgin flight
into uncharted territories.
The cycle is complete...
the madness understood...
and with this understanding, all has been
transformed into Love.
Life fulfills its own purpose
and celebrates itself.

Thank you, Quinten, for having come to me as my son; you are a great part of my celebration of life. Our journey has been delightful, our conversation has made itself manifest through our wordless connection, for it somehow found the wings to fly, and made us soar with joy and contentment.

May this be continued at some point in time...

Son:

What a great subject to finish on. So much of this book has been about day-to-day life, that this subject seems the perfect way to round it all off. First, I want to say thank you for inviting me on this book journey with you. It originally took me several months to respond to your invitation, but it always sat there, in the background, beckoning me to answer your call. And now that it's done, it feels so right. My soul has enjoyed this medium of expression thoroughly. Joining with you in this space of open, shared truth as experienced through our individual lives, has made it so much sweeter. Thank you, I adore you, I love you... always.

After reflecting on the subject of life for some days, the idea of choice has been coming up constantly, the choices that we make daily. There are big decisions that can change the course of a life, and then there are momentary choices that can simply change our mood or our day. I was on a mini road trip to Joshua Tree this past weekend with Ms. Lovely. I found myself, at times, getting into negative patterns of thought. They often, if not always, stemmed from that oh-so-nagging emotion of fear. Sometime during the process, I decided to make the choice to focus on the love. I chose to love my surroundings, love myself, love Ms. Lovely, sending her love, receiving her love, and focusing on positive things. I guess fear didn't like that, because it disappeared. Everything became more pleasant, more light, more beautiful, and easier. All I had to do was to choose what to let my soul ruminate on... fear or love. Such a simple choice that fully changed my experience of those days.

This lesson has continued in the days since that trip. I have found that so many events occur daily that I have the choice of how to respond. For example, yesterday I was playing golf with Dad. At one point in the round, somebody drove up right behind us precisely as I was about to hit my tee shot. It was quite distracting, but I tried to ignore it and swing anyways. Well, I hit a terrible shot. I was so annoyed with the bad shot and the disturbance, that I had my worst score on that hole for the day, and continued to play badly over the next couple of holes, still feeling irritation and blame. I then remembered the lessons from the weekend trip of choosing love and positivity. Now, it did feel good at some level to be upset and blame somebody else for my woes rather than take personal responsibility for my feelings. However, on a deeper level, I knew that these toxic feelings would lead to further unpleasantness reflected in my play and in my interactions with others. So, I chose to forget about it and enjoy each moment of the beautiful sunny day, the surrounding nature, and to focus on positive outcomes. Lo and behold, the next 9 holes turned out to be the best 9 holes of my life! I had never, at that point, scored so low on any 9 holes anywhere before. All it took was a simple choice of what to focus on. I have, for a long time, been a big believer in making choices from the heart, feeling my way through decisions in life. This conviction has mainly been in regards to larger moments. I haven't tried very much, though I have tried, to pay as much attention to the micro-decisions of day-to-day events and how those affect my mood, those around me, and my overall experience of life. So, this lesson could be a nice new tool to use and to play with, as you often do, to affect the momentary and daily inner responses to ordinary things and to convert experiences to more kindhearted and pleasant ones. What fun!

Pondering the above paragraph, I suppose that if I was more fully surrendered to the way of the heart, the path of love, that even these little daily choices would automatically be positive and loving ones. But as a human, dealing with my own levels of inconvenience in the form of occasional inner turmoil and self-sabotage, I have found it useful to observe my inner reactions and actively guide those responses to a more positive and loving focused direction. I do, however, want to clear up some things that I think could be a bit dangerous even with this mentality. A person could truly be in a situation that is no longer in service to one's higher self, and stay stuck in that place while trying to always bring love and positivity into that unhealthy experience rather than realizing that it would be more loving to be free from it. So, there are two things at play here: a positive and love focused approach to inner reactions, and a deeper inner guidance, the soul compass as it might be called. I'm guilty myself, many times over, of ignoring the discomfort of my soul, in favor of trying to give another what they want, or trying to make something work that just didn't. I've stayed in a few situations that my soul and my core guidance knew and could feel that were not right for me. I stayed in many of those situations longer than I probably should have. But I wasn't wise enough at those points to see things as clearly as I would have liked. Everything and every person in my life has taught me so much though, so I wouldn't change anything. *I'm eternally grateful and full of love for everyone that has crossed my path and helped me grow. The only thing that I'm trying to say is that, if I had the clarity that I have now, and a deeper trust in my inner being, that I could have avoided pain for myself and others. I may have tried to focus on love, but by ignoring my inner, deeper directives, I was not actually choosing love. I was choosing sacrifice. The loving choice for my life, as well as the life of others involved, was for me to be true to what my soul knew, at some level, to be true. And that was to stop trying to force something to work that simply did not. At times, the positive and loving decision is to set free that which doesn't serve our growth to its highest possible potential. Sometimes, we have to choose to honor ourselves and all involved by being true to an inner depth, a soul clarity. So, for me, for my life so far, I am finding that one of the major lessons that I'm learning is to trust those deep instincts ever more and more. The newest lesson that is arising is to actively choose positivity and love even in the smaller things. These two lessons seem to make for a more harmonious life overall and a better, more loving experience in the day-to-day life also.*

Every day, every moment, we have a choice of how to react, how to live, how to be. Any moment can be a moment that we choose to be the best version of ourselves. Love is always the right choice, whether that expresses as love for life, self, others, or all. Love is the choice from which to fully live. May we all, through courage, through perseverance, through humility, and through faith and guidance, find a way to express unconditional love as much as possible, to the fullest extent possible. Love heals me, love heals you, love heals all things. Love is the choice of life and life is the choice of Love.

Life

I've chosen to live, and through every choice,
I am woven to give, I release my voice.
Let me listen, let me choose...
hearts that glisten, I wish to peruse.
Show me how it shall be done,
to live in love, to live as One.
When we stumble, or we collapse,
let's be humble, not fall in traps.
Traps of mind, patterns that surface,
just be kind, love is the purpose.
The way is there, if we can find
upon the hallowed sands of time,
how to live in heart, not in mind.
Wafting through the waves of eternity,
does come faith and endless certainty,
that love and peace are true and actually,
the way that life is lived quite naturally.
I've said love so very many times,

through paragraphs and little rhymes.
I'll say it again and again,
through many words and lines,
To family or friends,
of yours and mine,
to strangers and foes,
and to all of those,
until my heart grows
and until all existence knows

That LOVE LOVE LOVE
is how all life flows!

I love you Quinten…
I love you, Mother…

Connect with us at:
CaruthConversations.com

Made in the USA
Columbia, SC
01 December 2021

50036030R00098